GREATER

Raleigh Court

Mayor Nelson Harris

GREATER

Raleigh Court

A HISTORY OF
WASENA, VIRGINIA HEIGHTS,
NORWICH & RALEIGH COURT

Nelson Harris

Charleston London

History
PRESS

Published by The History Press
Charleston, SC 29403
www.historypress.net

Cover image: Grandin Theater and Brice's Drugstore, taken by George Davis on July 16, 1946. *Courtesy of HSWV.*

First published 2007

Manufactured in the United Kingdom

ISBN 978.1.59629.235.2

Library of Congress CIP data applied for.

To Cathy

CONTENTS

ACKNOWLEDGEMENTS

As with all books, authors must rely upon the generous assistance and support of other persons and organizations. It is my pleasure to note with great appreciation the following for their support of my efforts. Thanks to the staff of the Virginia Room at the Roanoke Public Library's Main Branch, namely Brenda Finley, Laura Wickstead, Pam Young and Alicia Sell. I am also grateful to the two historical societies in the Roanoke Valley for use of their photo archives: to Kent Chrisman and the Historical Society of Western Virginia, and John Long and the Salem Historical Society. Two fine gentlemen who provided me good counsel in the history of Raleigh Court were the Honorable Robert Garland, former member of Roanoke City Council, and the Honorable James Brice, a retired judge. I am also grateful to the various churches that responded to my requests for their histories, which have been incorporated as a separate chapter in the book. I also appreciate access to the photo archives of the Virginia Heights Baptist Church and Christ Lutheran Church. Finally, I would offer thanks to my father, Charlie Harris, for his guidance and knowledge as a lifelong resident of the Raleigh Court area.

There are a number of archival photographs used throughout the book. Credits are initialized and represent the following organizations: Salem Historical Society (SHS), Historical Society of Western Virginia (HSWV), Roanoke Public Library (RPL), Christ Lutheran Church (CLC), Virginia Heights Baptist Church (VHBC), Robert Garland (Garland) and the Virginia Museum of Transportation (VMT).

INTRODUCTION

The year 2007 is special in many ways. It is the 125th anniversary of the city of Roanoke, and it is also the centennial of the Greater Raleigh Court neighborhood. I am the mayor of Roanoke and a lifelong resident of Raleigh Court, so these anniversaries occur at unique moments in my civic life. Consequently, researching and writing this book were personal pleasures, albeit challenging ones.

The story of Raleigh Court is in many ways the story of Roanoke itself. The neighborhood was annexed into the city in 1919, but had already seen much development and interaction with the city prior to annexation. Like many residential developments of this period, there were exclusions as to whom could move into Virginia Heights, Wasena and Raleigh Court that blemish their histories, but these neighborhoods have matured and developed over the years to encompass a diversity of residents and traditions.

Of particular interest is the history of Norwich. Being an industrial center on the outskirts of Roanoke in the late 1880s, Norwich and its citizens suffered greatly through the turbulent economic times of the 1890s and through the first several years of the next century. Norwich was the site of factories erected by Roanoke's leading capitalists, yet those same factories were surrounded by tenement housing. Child laborers struggled in the cotton mill with no one to champion their cause locally to receive healthcare or a basic education. Yet it was in Norwich that public education had its roots in this section of the city. It was to Norwich that the first street railway cars carried persons from downtown to beyond the city limit. It was in Norwich that floods, fires and other tragedies struck, but her residents demonstrated time and again a resiliency to rise above such events. While Grandin Road may boast the grand homes, Norwich contains the stories of human inspiration and triumph over adversity.

Raleigh Court, like the city itself, is the beneficiary of the civic efforts of many. Most notable was the Fishburn family, whose donation of lands created the major parks now enjoyed by residents of the Greater Raleigh Court area. In addition to the Fishburns, Greater Raleigh Court has been shaped by the small businessmen and women who opened on Grandin Road, Main Street and Bridge Street the groceries, barbershops, hardware stores, drugstores, beauty salons, restaurants, dry cleaners and retail shops.

Introduction

While some only stayed for a year or two, others became fixtures in the memories of longtime residents due to their decades-long presences in the commercial villages of Greater Raleigh Court.

Greater Raleigh Court boasts numerous amenities today that are not present in other neighborhoods. No one can think about Greater Raleigh Court without commenting on the presence and importance of Roanoke's last remaining neighborhood theater, the Grandin. Today, Grandin Road has expanded sidewalks with outdoor diners, and the storefronts are complete with shops, restaurants and retailers as always.

This is not to say that Greater Raleigh Court has not experienced its challenges. Older housing stock, considered by some a liability, is now back in vogue, with homebuyers appreciating the diversity of architectural styles and craftsmanship not present in modern construction. The tree-lined streets where oaks, maples and sycamores drape their limbs across the road create a green canopy in spring and summer and a collage of color in fall.

There are the renovated old schools, Wasena and Virginia Heights, which still have their eight-decade-old façades. These are joined now by the modern, newly rebuilt Patrick Henry High School, which speaks of a renewed commitment to and investment in public education.

One cannot know whether the early real estate developers and land companies had any idea that their efforts would eventually create the Greater Raleigh Court experienced by residents and visitors today. What is known, and what I have tried to document, is that the Greater Raleigh Court of today is due to the attentive and thoughtful efforts of citizens, city officials, business owners, faith groups, civic leagues and other organizations to create a residential community that is envied and honored.

For the purposes of my research, I have focused upon four main neighborhoods: Norwich, Wasena, Virginia Heights and Raleigh Court. While the name Greater Raleigh Court may seem to some to be favoritism, it is not. It is my way of simply referring to these sections that make up the oldest part of southwest Roanoke City, post-1919. I have touched upon some developments that occurred outside these neighborhoods, but only because I felt they impacted Greater Raleigh Court and should be included for that reason.

The book is written chronologically, so that the reader might have a better sense of the progression of these neighborhoods over the years. While it may not make for sterling narrative, it will hopefully allow readers to quickly find and put in context various events and moments within the progression of time.

With the exception of college and graduate school, I have lived all of my life in the Raleigh Court area. It is a special place, because it is home. And that, as the old proverb states, is where one's heart is. Thus, I commend this centennial history to each reader in the hope that it might inform, enlighten and inspire all those who will carry forward the tending and care of this place called Roanoke and its many neighborhoods.

Chapter 1

A Splendid Suburb

When the editor for the *Roanoke Times* penned the headline for the Sunday morning, January 21, 1906 edition, he probably had little notion as to the prophetic nature of his words: "City to Have Splendid Suburb." The subtitle explained the matter succinctly: "Land Beyond Norwich Bridge to be Laid Off Into Lots and Streets."

The newspaper was noting the purchase of some one hundred acres in Roanoke County, just across the river from the city, by the development firm of Bellamy, Hough and Hardy. This firm was well known in the urban areas of Virginia, having developed middle- and upper-income neighborhoods in both Richmond and Norfolk. Of interest to Roanokers was the firm's most recent development of the Ghent neighborhood in the 1890s in Norfolk, where Bellamy, Hough and Hardy was located. According to plans released by J.W. Hough, one of the partners, the acreage of this new development was to be divided into lots 50 by 130 feet, each of them facing on a wide street and to be offered for sale for residential purposes only. Streets would be graded, granolithic walks were to be laid on all the streets and a comprehensive sewer system was to be installed. The *Times* further reported, "The section will have electric lights and every modern convenience."

J.W. Hough's firm would be represented locally by Stras, Walton & Company of Roanoke City. Even the *Norfolk Dispatch* commented on the transaction and its potential for Roanoke: "Mr. J.W. Hough…returned from Roanoke, Va., this morning, where he closed a deal for 100 acres of Roanoke city suburban property which his firm will convert into the 'Ghent' of Roanoke. Closely following the recent deal of a similar nature which his firm made in Richmond, it would seem that they intend extending their business indefinitely and regardless of territory."[1]

Realtors T. Marshall Bellamy and J. Thomas Hough had been quite successful in Norfolk, having developed a number of subdivisions, including Ghent. When the history of that Norfolk development is traced, one can understand the origin for the use of the "Ghent" name in Roanoke. The Norfolk subdivision of Ghent was developed on a large farm that had once belonged to Jasper Moran. Local tradition stated that Moran, who had purchased the land in 1810, named his tract "Ghent" a few years thereafter to commemorate the signing of the famous treaty ending the War of 1812. That treaty was of great importance to the Norfolk area, as it reopened the sea lanes after years of embargo. Moran's farm was acquired in 1890 by the Norfolk Company, which retained Moran's name for the tract. Thus, Bellamy and Hough imported the "Ghent" name to Roanoke, having developed property with that title in Norfolk.[2] This partnership of Norfolk and Roanoke interests became the Roanoke-Ghent Realty Company.

Within one week of the Bellamy, Hough and Hardy announcement came another. This one, made by the Clyndale Land Company of Roanoke, informed that some two hundred acres owned by the company were to be divided into suburban lots. The *Roanoke Times* described the Clyndale property and plan as follows:

> *These two hundred acres owned by the Clyndale Company adjoin the Solitude farm, and have an elevation that commands a full sweep view of Roanoke and the country for many miles in all directions. It is reached from the city via the Virginia Avenue [later* Memorial Avenue] *bridge which spans the Roanoke River. The tract is only one-quarter of a mile from the river bridge—not more than eight minutes walk from that point, or from Norwich—and it is only twenty minutes drive from the Terry Building, or the center of Roanoke's business district. The Roanoke Railway and Electric Company operates street cars across the Virginia Avenue bridge and on out to Norwich, thus making the Clyndale site easily accessible.*

Clyndale was selling lots for between $150 and $200. Clyndale also put no restrictions on the kinds of homes to be erected. "If a party wishes to build a home costing $2,000, all right; if it is desired to erect a house costing $15,000, all right—and so much the better. But the Clyndale Company will not bind a buyer to any promise, so far as the cost of the house goes. The idea simply is to build up a healthy suburban village that will be composed of progressive citizens," reported the *Times*. The real estate firm of Turner & Thomas of Roanoke City served as the exclusive agents for Clyndale.[3]

One should note that in the late nineteenth and early twentieth centuries, many cities were experiencing significant suburban development. Developers were typically using a grid formula popularly known as City Beautiful, which had emerged during the Chicago World's Fair. The land to be known largely as Raleigh Court was attractive to developers for three main reasons. First, there was existing trolley access, specifically from the city across Virginia Avenue bridge. Second, there were three bridges spanning the Roanoke River into the area—Norwich Bridge, Virginia Avenue Bridge and Wasena Bridge. These bridges were rather primitive and would be replaced with the larger bridges seen today, but they did mitigate the river as being a barrier. Third, by building outside the city on adjoining lands, developers could often skirt building codes and regulations, knowing soon-to-follow annexation would make it city property eventually.

Developers also used an aggressive marketing campaign, often with a European flavor. Wide streets with grand homes (at least compared to those in the city) and names such as Windsor, Arlington, Sherwood, Avon, etc., gave the new neighborhoods an appealing romanticism.

The Wasena Land Company came into being in 1909 and purchased the farm of George Howbert on January 2, 1910, for $60,000. While history gives no indication as to the rationale for the name "Wasena," the term is a word from a Native American language meaning "beautiful view." (The street name Winona is also Native American in origin.) The land company began with certain immediate changes, namely the replacement of an old ore railroad bridge with a larger steel structure in 1911, along with street grading and the subdivision of residential lots. The erection of a steel bridge by the land company was necessary, as the only bridge in the vicinity at that time was a narrow-gauge railroad bridge that once served a small ore mine operation run by Ferdinand Rorer. This bridge was given to a company to dismantle in exchange for salvaging from it the steel and timber. Just prior to World War I, the stone abutments of this old bridge were dynamited.

An advertisement by the Wasena Land Company in the August 24, 1912 edition of the *Roanoke Evening World* read as follows:

> *Right to the Front: Wasena is moving ahead. Where is Wasena? It is a beautiful suburb lying on Roanoke River and gently sloping ground beyond, with a wonderful view and delightful mountain air. It is close in, too; right at the terminus of the Highland car line, with a magnificent bridge connecting it directly with the older portion of the city. All modern conveniences have been provided, sewers, sidewalks, lights, water, telephones. Building actively in Wasena is more in evidence than in any other suburban section.*

The same ad also listed for sale the "old Howbert homestead" with two and a half acres, a good house, outhouses and a spring of pure water. A price was available upon request.

All of this activity caught the attentive eye of realtor Ronnie R. Fairfax, who at the time was successfully selling lots in Villa Heights and Waverly Place. He, in turn, formed the Wasena Corporation in 1916 and added the new subdivision to his interests, employing a number of salesmen who offered lots in Wasena for two dollars down and the same thereafter each week. By 1917, the first few blocks near the new bridge were developed and occupied.[4]

The Metropolitan Land Corporation filed a plat in June of 1907 that was known as the Metropolitan Heights Addition. The month before, the Virginia Heights Corporation had filed its plat as well. Interestingly, many of the streets laid out by Metropolitan had original names much different from the present. Belleville and Arden were named Lafayette Place and Triton Place, respectively. Some streets were to have landscaped medians. When these medians were never developed, this left some streets with lot sizes much larger than their cross-street counterparts. Arden was Grant Street, Carter was Liberty Street, a portion of Belleville was Paris Street, Laburnum was Roosevelt and Avenel was Filmore. Many of these names were changed to their current titles when the Raleigh Court Corporation purchased the Metropolitan Land Corporation's subdivision in 1910.[5]

Bridge Street in Norwich, 1928. *Courtesy of SHS.*

The seeds for the development of Greater Raleigh Court had really been sown about a decade prior to the announcements of the land development companies with the industrialization of Norwich. In 1890, James S. Simmons of the Roanoke Development Company announced some $1.1 million worth of capital stock, mostly purchased by Northern investors. With a portion of those resources, much of what is now Norwich was acquired. About this same time, the Norfolk and Western Railway was completing a belt line connecting Norwich to present-day Franklin Road.

Prior to these significant developments, Norwich had been largely cornfields on the William Persinger family farm, known as Turkey Bottom. With the purchase of the land by the Roanoke Development Company, the area was supposedly called "Norwich" in honor of Charles E. Beebe, first president of the Norwich Lock Company, who was from Norwich, Connecticut. The area was ripe for commercial development due to the proximity of the West End Furnace located across the river, coupled with anticipated rail access. The developers laid out a plat delineating both residential and industrial sites. Cottages were erected to accommodate laborers, segregated by race—whites only, with blacks residing across the river—and a bridge was constructed at the present site of Bridge Street. Shortly thereafter, companies began locating in Norwich: Norwich Lock Company (later the Roanoke Cotton Mill and then the Twine Mill), the Duval Engine Company, Shelf Hardware, Cushion Iron Works and the Bridgewater Carriage Company.

The Bridgewater Carriage Company moved into Norwich from its former location on the northwest corner of Church Avenue and First Street. At that location, it occupied a three-story brick building where it was one of the leading manufacturers of carriages and other horse-drawn equipment. The carriage company had been chartered in

Row houses in Norwich, 1928. *Courtesy of SHS.*

Roanoke in November 1889, with P.S. Miller as president. By 1891, the enterprise had moved to Norwich. The carriage company would be short-lived. The economic depression of the late 1890s led to its demise, and the company's assets were sold at public auction in 1894. (Coincidentally, the company's first building on Church Avenue burned that same year.)[6]

The Norwich Lock Company opened in 1891, and on its first day produced eight tons of castings. The Lock Company would be another victim of the depression of the late nineteenth century. By 1898, it was bankrupt and sold for a paltry $6,500, in comparison to its original cost of $125,000. The purchaser was a local attorney, Hamilton Graves. Later that same year, the Lock Company was utilized by the Roanoke Hardware Company, which hoped to profitably reemploy some two hundred men in the manufacturing of locks. This did not occur, and by year's end the Lock Company changed hands for a third time, being sold to some Lynchburg investors for $25,000. One year later, it was announced that a cotton mill would occupy the Lock Company's site, which it did in 1901.[7]

Noted Roanoke historian Raymond Barnes described the early days of Norwich:

> *Into the little cottages poured the workman and the prospect of receiving hard money for 10 hours work each day was entrancing. Many had brought with them their life savings, or the proceeds of a little farm. Some put their all into a little cottage for the future looked fair…Norwich residents zealously guarded their territory and a boy from another section of town was like unto a strange dog in a new neighborhood. Many an innocent fisherman wandering into Norwich territory received such a warm reception he departed in haste accompanied on his journey with rocks, hoots and yells.*[8]

Housing conditions outside the cotton mill in Norwich, May 1911. *Courtesy of RPL.*

For all of its immediate success, Norwich suffered greatly in 1891 as the Roanoke River moved out of its banks, as it would do often, and into Norwich, flooding homes and washing away outbuildings.

With the population of Norwich increasing and commercial enterprises growing, the Roanoke Street Railway Company extended its West End Line in 1891 down Roanoke Avenue and across Bridge Street. The following year, the line (later named Norwich Branch) was electrified.

In 1893, the national economy collapsed, and Norwich bore the full brunt. A financial panic sent the U.S. economy into its worst depression in history. Railroads went bankrupt and the New York Stock Exchange went on a selling spree. By the end of that year, some five hundred banks and fifteen thousand business firms had fallen into bankruptcy. What many thought would be temporary dragged on for four years.

The Bridgewater Carriage Company did not survive and was sold at auction in 1894. Three years later, the Duval Engine Works in Norwich went bankrupt and its capital assets were sold at public auction for $11,000. For three years, vacant laborer cottages in Norwich were sold to investors who had the homes physically moved to more prosperous sections of the city and resold for handsome profits. Meanwhile, the working men of Norwich saw their meager wages cut consistently. According to historian Barnes, Norwich soon resembled a beleaguered Northern mill town.

By the end of 1896, many in Norwich were destitute. In a holiday appeal to its readership, the *Roanoke Times* ran a revealing story after being prompted by J.J. Cox, proprietor of the St. James Hotel and a member of the Elk's Christmas tree committee, who escorted the *Times* reporter through Norwich. The journalist's observations were stark:

> *If ever a place was cursed with wretchedness, poverty and suffering, it is the place in question. The starved, pinched faces of the poverty stricken women and children are there to speak for themselves, and can be investigated by any who care to look into the matter…The first home reached was occupied by an old man and his wife with six or seven children among them being two daughters nearly grown. They are without fuel except such as can be picked up along the river banks and in the outlying woodland, possibly a mile or more away. The husband and father is ill and unable to work, and the extent of their stores is a little cornmeal and less than a pound of fat bacon. The first coffee that they have had in a long time burned yesterday while being roasted. The family needs to be assisted. They want something to eat and fuel to keep warm…The next house investigated consisted of a husband and wife and seven or eight small children, many of the little fellows barefooted and their clothing thin and worn. They were in poor shape so far as fuel was concerned, but it seems they have been enabled through the work of the husband to keep actual want from the door. They have been placed in a bad fix for the winter owing to the recent confinement of the husband in the city jail for a misdemeanor and the sickness of the mother. A little charity bestowed on this family would not be amiss…Another family visited was that of a widow with six children, the youngest just*

two years old. She has struggled to support her little ones by taking in washing and by sewing and such other work as she could obtain. Her children are small and mostly girls, all bright children, but they are now facing a cruel, cold winter. The mother had managed to provide comfortable clothing for the children, with the exception of shoes, but now for three days they have had no bread except what they borrowed from a neighbor. They are out of fuel and perhaps enough fat meat to last them through the day. If ever there was an object worthy of charity, surely this family is…Another family living in the same row are almost in similar circumstances so far as their immediate needs are concerned. They may not be as worthy of charity as others, but the suffering, little children are not responsible for their present condition…The last place visited was a house which has many broken windows and has a cold, cheerless appearance. The reporter entered and found seated within the room and around a small egg stove, a mother and seven children ranging in age from 13 years down to two weeks old infant which the mother held in her arms. The fire was poor, and hunger was plainly depicted on the faces of the children. The articles of furniture consisted of three pieces of chairs, two small benches, and an old dilapidated lounge, with a dirty quilt covering it. The children were barefooted, dirty and their hair was disheveled and unkempt. In an adjoining room were two beds or makeshifts for beds, with poor coverings, an old broken up cook stove and a small pine table. This seemed to be the entire store of this family. They were living, no not living, but existing in poverty, filth and wretchedness that is hard to contemplate without seeing for yourself.[9]

The article concluded with an appeal to inquire about making charitable contributions to the families at the St. James Hotel. Such was the standard of living for many in Norwich after nearly four years of economic depression.

In 1899, a tornado touched down in Norwich, destroying the community's only church, Woodside Chapel. On August 12 at 4:30 in the afternoon, rain poured for half an hour, immobilizing the trains at the passenger station downtown. While little damage was noted in the city proper, the *Roanoke Times* reported,

The wind struck Norwich from the northwest and blew in the stack house of the West End furnace and did other minor damage. The chief havoc, however, was Woodside Presbyterian Church building which was completely demolished. It was said last night that the building was nothing more than kindling wood and that the organ and other contents were also ruined…The little church is nothing more than a pile of twisted timbers, the whole structure before being crushed being lifted five or six feet from the floor and foundation. The north wall was blown out and turned upside down with the inside facing out. Large timbers were twisted into splinters one hundred feet from the foundation, and lathes and plaster and other debris so obstructed the road one hundred yards away that they had to be cleared away before wagons could pass. The building appeared to be taken up in a whirlwind and twisted all to pieces…A large number of people went out to the ruined church last night and in the afternoon. Those residents of Norwich who were in the habit of worshipping there were deeply moved, especially the children, who shed tears freely.[10]

Russell Avenue in Norwich, 1928. *Courtesy of SHS.*

For all the damage sustained by the Woodside Chapel, there was one story that emerged that seemed miraculous, as explained by the *Roanoke Times*: "A strange thing connected with the destruction of the church was that not a Bible was injured to the slightest extent, while everything else, including the organ and furniture were utterly ruined. The large Bible was found with the smaller ones under a cloth used as a sort of partition in the church. A big cross had fallen upon them and protected them from the rain."[11]

The Woodside Chapel was the first and only church in Norwich at that time. A frame building with a seating capacity of 350 persons, it had been a mission of Roanoke's First Presbyterian Church. Costing $1,000 to construct, the chapel was erected in 1891 and had weathered the uneven economic decade and its toll upon the Norwich section. The local reporter was obviously moved by the church's role in the community when he noted, "It has been pre-eminently a children's church, and the only church that many of them have ever known. It was touching to see them on Saturday, after the storm, gather about the wreck and pick up the pieces of the broken organ and pile them together with as much tenderness as they would have cared for some living thing." The Woodside Chapel was not insured against tornado damage; thus, the members could do little more than clear the debris. The congregation, however, was given temporary worship space by nearby Methodists. An outstanding debt of $50 remained on the chapel, but Norwich residents were certainly in no position to satisfy it. At the next Sunday service of First Presbyterian, the pastor spoke to the matter before his people and in a few minutes ten members of that congregation voluntarily gave $5 each to meet the obligation. Woodside Chapel would eventually bounce back, but the lone church of Norwich had suffered greatly.[12]

Roanoke Avenue in Norwich, 1928. *Courtesy of SHS.*

Interestingly, there were some significant plans for Norwich that never materialized. For example, the Roanoke Land Development Company had originally plotted for a hotel to be constructed at the end of Denniston Avenue to complement their initial design for Norwich. With the N&W belt line, some had even made room in Norwich for its own train station. Most notable, however, were discussions by civic leaders in 1901 to consider Norwich as the site for the city's fairgrounds. After much deliberation, city officials decided on land west of Jefferson Street. A few years later, the fairgrounds were relocated a short distance away to present-day Reserve Avenue, eventually becoming home to Maher Field and later Victory Stadium.

Public education in Raleigh Court also had its beginnings as a result of the industries and workers in Norwich. Given that annexation would not come until 1919, the first twenty-five years of public education for the Norwich–Virginia Heights section were provided by Roanoke County. The county school board minutes and ledgers for this time period indicate that the first public school for the section, Norwich, opened for the 1892–93 school year as school No. 8 in the Big Lick School District. That first year, Florence Ribble was the teacher. She had seventy-one students enrolled, with an average daily attendance of thirty-two. As compulsory attendance was years in the future, most county schools had daily average attendance at about half of the enrollment. According to county school records, the Norwich School (not to be confused with the school that would later be built by Roanoke City in Norwich) had the following faculty and enrollment (average daily attendance):

Virginia Heights Elementary School, 1922. In the foreground is the foundation being laid for Virginia Heights Baptist Church. *Courtesy of VHBC.*

1893–94	Mattie Britt, Beatrice Agnew;	49 students (23)
1894–95	Mattie Britt, Jennie Moore;	119 students (59)
1895–96	Mattie Britt, Jennie Moore;	100 students (65)
1896–97	R.E. Cook, Jennie Moore;	106 students (56)
1897–98	Giles Gunn, Mamie Bush;	102 students (53)
1898–99	Jennie Moore;	58 students (35)
1899–1900	J.P. Haislip, Giles Gunn, Eula Merriman, Mamie Barksdale;	73 students (43)
1900–01	Virginia Gurrant, Lottie Walker;	63 students (44)
1901–02	Reverend John Lips, Eulalie Starritt;	85 students (39)

County school records are missing for the years between 1902 and 1909, which is unfortunate because it is believed that in 1906 the first brick schoolhouse was constructed on the site of the current Virginia Heights Elementary School. This four-room building was used for almost eighty years at the school and is well remembered by local residents who attended Virginia Heights. It was razed in 1984. School records do show that in 1911, the name of school No. 8 was changed from "Norwich" to "Virginia Heights." This probably was not the result of a change in location, but simply reflected the development that was occurring at that time and that the section was more commonly referred to as Virginia Heights.

Prior to the construction of the small brick school building in 1906, Virginia Heights School was housed in a little, gray, one-room schoolhouse that sat on the back of the present-day school lot.

Between 1909 and annexation in 1919, the Norwich–Virginia Heights School No. 8 was served by the following, for various periods, as members of the faculty: Villa Marshall, Murrell Correll, Florence Obenchain, Mary Brice, Gertie Bowers, Mrs. Katherine Averill, Margaret Brown, Marion Walker, Hattie Bernard, Kate Bulman, Mary Watson, Ocie Stiff, Helen Bulman, Mrs. M.L. Keister, Bettie Ellis, Mrs. Nora Ashworth, Salome Moomaw, Grace Dickenson, Mary Frantz, Helen Frantz, Frances Repass, Edna Bulman, Kathleen Baker, Rachel Garrett, Fannie Moffett, Elizabeth Parr, Elizabeth Cooke, Mary Nelms, Dora Almond, Mrs. W.T. Ross, Mrs. N.Y. Weeks, Claudine Avent and Mrs. C.N. Garner. During this period, enrollment grew steadily, as did attendance. In 1909–10, the enrollment for the school was 96, with an average daily attendance of 51. By the 1918–19 school year, enrollment was 404 with an average daily attendance of 243. The faculty grew from 2 teachers in 1909 to 11 by 1919.[13]

Another development during this ten-year period was the increase in the number of instructional days. In 1909–10, the school year consisted of 142 days, and by 1919 the school calendar had 180 days. This additional month came as the result of interest from within the Virginia Heights community. An article in the *Roanoke Times* on September 2, 1915, was headlined "Longer School for Va. Heights." It read, in part,

A considerable amount of debate pro and con on the question of making the school term at Virginia Heights nine instead of eight months, featured a well-attended and interesting meeting of the citizens of that flourishing community last evening. The extra month was decided upon, however, despite some opposition, and a committee will get to work on subscriptions from patrons in that section and will report to another citizens meeting…According to the school board, which is willing to finance half of the necessary expense, it will be necessary for the patrons to raise the other half, and the committee will proceed to raise this amount by subscription among its citizens who will be benefited by a longer school term.

The opposition to the extra month which developed at the meeting last night was based not on the expense, but on the futility of conducting a nine-month school in what are said to be too limited quarters. The Virginia Heights School has but five teachers and five rooms and has to provide room and instruction for some three hundred pupils.

There is some talk among patrons of raising enough money to provide more room, but whether the plan will be carried into execution is not yet known.

The efforts of parents and others proved successful. Beginning September 7, 1915, the school year was extended to nine months for Virginia Heights. Interestingly, this decision seemed to be motivated by a desire to replicate the city's calendar. Given that the vast majority of Virginia Heights residents had relocated to their suburb from the city, they probably had become accustomed to the nine-month course of study and may have felt their students were being shortchanged by a county system that had not implemented the longer term. This is evidenced by the fact that at the citizens meeting, Roanoke City Superintendent Harris Hart delivered an address entitled "The Benefits Derived From a City Course of Study in a Nine Months' School." On a side note, at the same meeting the school's new principal, Miss Ocie Stiff, spoke about "The Tests of a Good Community," and the gathering was entertained by Miss Maude Lower on the piano and Mr. Holland Persinger, violinist.[14]

The development of Norwich and the general need for county residents to access the city limits brought forward the construction, in 1891, of the Virginia Avenue Bridge (also called Woodrum Bridge), the predecessor of the Memorial Bridge. While it is uncertain when exactly the Virginia Avenue Bridge opened, city council records reflect that by 1897 the bridge was in need of repair. That summer, council authorized expenditures for the repair and painting of the bridge and came to an agreement with Roanoke County that they would maintain the viaduct on their side of the Roanoke River. C.A. Berry was awarded the $276 contract. A year later, however, the city engineer determined that the bridge needed new joists and flooring, with the specific recommendation that steel joists replace the wooden ones and that the wood-plank sidewalks be removed. The Virginia Bridge and Iron Company was awarded a contract to make general repairs. While the city paid for most of the work, costs were also reimbursed to the city by Roanoke County and the Roanoke Street Railway Company. Work was completed by mid-January 1899. These repairs kept the bridge operable for fifteen more years.

Virginia Avenue Bridge, 1915. *Courtesy of HSWV.*

Workers in Roanoke Cotton Mills, Norwich, 1911. *Courtesy of RPL.*

Another interesting development worth noting about the bridge and river was a recommendation forwarded to the city council by Roanoke's mayor in a letter dated July 5, 1898. The mayor stated,

> *A number of boys persist in bathing in the streams adjacent to the city, a practice that with the present police force is impossible to prevent. Many of them out of fear of being arrested are now bathing in Tinker Creek, and while this is secluded, it is polluted by the refuse of the slaughter pens above, as well as the whole of the city sewage. Should the police force succeed in preventing the practice at this point, the boys, no doubt, would repair to the deeper waters of the river, with the consequent danger of some of them being drowned. Three were drowned two years ago. To prevent this danger, as well as the bathing in public places, I would recommend that [council] have a section east of the Virginia Avenue Bridge designated and suitably prepared for bathing.*

Council concurred.

One of the saddest chapters in the history and development of the Greater Raleigh Court area was the employment of child laborers in Norwich. In 1900, city leaders were pursuing the establishment of a cotton mill. Cotton mills had served the economies of other localities throughout the South and New England, and there was an expanding market for cotton in China at the turn of the century. Unfortunately, the cotton industry, like others, depended upon the exploitation of child workers to produce low-cost goods. Within Virginia, the child labor abolitionists had not gained strength enough to stop such employment practices. Lynchburg and Richmond both had cotton mills with child workers, and bills introduced into the Virginia General Assembly to regulate the employment of children met with strong and effective opposition from local boards of trade.

One bill, introduced in the Session of 1900, stipulated that no child under the age of ten shall be employed in factories and that no child under the age of sixteen shall be employed in factories unless they had attended school for three months during the year preceding their employment. Further, no child should be employed more than forty-eight hours per week. This bill was swiftly and adamantly opposed, suffering a quick legislative death. Joining the opposition to the bill was Roanoke's board of trade.

During the discussion of the legislation, the *Roanoke Times* offered the following comment:

> *In so far as the provision that no child under ten years of age shall be employed in factories is concerned, we believe it to be wise, as children under the age of ten are too young to begin the struggle of life in institutions of that kind. But we cannot agree that the rest of the bill is good. The educational stance smacks much of compulsory schooling, a point which this country has not yet and probably never will arrive. Education is an undisputed advantage and whenever possible should, and no doubt is, sought after, but*

Young spooler in cotton mill in Norwich, 1911. *Courtesy of RPL.*

there are conditions in life that cannot be gotten around in which bread is more important than schooling. It cannot be claimed that in any community parents will, as a general thing, take their children from school and put them to work, unless there is a necessity for it...there are thousands of families dependent largely upon their aid in getting bread that their children can give, and many whose struggles for existence are made much harder by the absence of opportunity for their children in their community. Life is real and earnest for them and the struggle for bread of greater importance than that for education...Were child labor restricted one of the chief advantages to be gained by such enterprises as this, vis; that of giving work to needy boys and girls would be destroyed and the industries themselves destroyed.[15]

During this same period, a headline appeared in the *Roanoke Times*, "Let Us Have A Cotton Mill!" The article opined as follows:

A splendid opportunity is now offered to Roanoke to have a cotton mill in her midst. The circumstances connected with the proposition are of the most favorable character. One of the first expenses that confronts a company organizing a cotton mill is the expenditures of $25,000 to $50,000 for a building. The Norwich Lock Works building which cost originally $60,000, or $75,000, is offered to the company for $10,000. The men who own the building are stockholders in the cotton mill in Lynchburg.

This description proved correct, as the Norwich Lock Works was sold to cotton interest for conversion of the building into the Roanoke Cotton Mill.

The Roanoke Cotton Mill (later the Twine Mill) employed child laborers, many of whom lived with their families in tenement housing within sight of the mill. Their conditions were in some cases squalid. For over a decade, children worked in Norwich's mill, but then they were discovered by a little-known photographer who made them his subjects, along with other child laborers across the South, in his campaign to end child labor.

Lewis Hine was a New York City schoolteacher and photographer. Reform-minded, Hine knew the value of photography in communicating a powerful story. Deeply moved by the plight of child laborers, Hine quit his teaching job to become an investigative photographer for the National Child Labor Committee. He traveled the country with an old-fashioned box camera photographing children at work. Motivated by the belief that if persons could see the abuses and injustice of child industrial workers they would demand its end, Hine went to coal mines, alleged vocational schools, laundries, slums and mills throughout the country. Then one day, in 1911, Hine came to Norwich and focused his lens on the children of the Roanoke Cotton Mill. How many photographs he took that day is unknown, but ten are now housed in the Hine's collection of the Library of Congress. Those photographs show the children of Norwich working the mill machinery; some are as young as seven. One group photograph captured a variety of expressions, but a close look reveals a childhood that is not so much lost as never gained.

The children of Norwich worked in the Roanoke Cotton Mill for some thirty years. While the abolishment of child labor was asserted many times, it was not until the Great Depression of the 1930s that adults needing employment displaced children. Finally, the Federal Fair Labor Standards Act of 1938 prohibited the employment of children under the age of sixteen in manufacturing and mining. Hine died in 1940 in much the same circumstance of his subjects—penniless and obscure.[16]

Thus, by the time the land development companies made their announcements in 1906 about new suburbs to be known as Ghent and Virginia Heights, the small, close-knit community of Norwich had already experienced an interesting and, at times, difficult history.

Between 1906 and 1920, a number of land development companies and real estate partnerships came into being that planned and developed the Greater Raleigh Court area. Many merged and others had subsidiaries, the relationships of which are often difficult to trace. Among the major firms during this period that expanded and developed the area were the following:

EVERGREEN DEVELOPMENT COMPANY—located at 6 Campbell Avenue Southeast, and incorporated in 1915, with C.M. Armes, president; and J.R. Ford, secretary-treasurer.

GHENT HEIGHTS LAND COMPANY—located at 204 Market Square and incorporated in 1910, with officers H.H. Markley, president; E.L. Moir, vice-president; and D.W. Persinger, secretary-treasurer.

METROPOLITAN HEIGHTS CORPORATION—operated from the Watt and Clay Building downtown and incorporated in 1907, with J.A. Strapf, president; and M.A. Riffe, vice-president.

RALEIGH COURT CORPORATION—headquartered in the Terry Building, with Gustavus Ober, president; James P. Woods, vice-president; M.A. Plunkett, secretary-treasurer; and Charles Beller, assistant treasurer.

RALEIGH INVESTMENT CORPORATION—J.P. Woods, president; R.H. Angell, vice-president; and J.L. Cook, secretary-treasurer.

ROANOKE-GHENT REALTY COMPANY—headquartered at 218 Jefferson Street, incorporated in 1906, with officers J.W. Hough, president; A.D.W. Walton, vice-president; and J. Stras, secretary-treasurer.

VIRGINIA HEIGHTS CORPORATION—located in the Watt and Clay Building and incorporated in 1905 with M.A. Riffe, president; M.C. Ellis, vice-president; C.C. Ellis, secretary; and J.T. Bandy, treasurer.

WASENA CORPORATION—headquartered at 302 South Jefferson, with R.R. Fairfax, president; H.R. Fairfax, vice-president; and I.E. Redmond, secretary-treasurer.[17]

WASENA LAND COMPANY—operated from the National Exchange Bank Building, with P.S. Miller, president; H.C. Barnes, vice-president; and Junius McGehee, secretary-treasurer.

The influence of these development companies cannot be underestimated, as they are responsible for the street layout and names that now define the area. The vast majority of street names were developed for reasons of marketing, as has already been suggested

Norwich, 1928. *Courtesy of SHS.*

earlier in the text. Others were named for early landowners or farmers of the area whose property was developed. Dudding Street was named for James Dudding, an area farmer; Persinger for John Persinger and his descendants, who owned vast lands in the Greater Raleigh Court area; Howbert for the Howbert family, whose farm consumed most of what later became Wasena. The most interesting naming story, however, is an urban legend relative to Grandin Road. Judge James Brice, a longtime Raleigh Court resident, related that in his younger years he was told by a longtime resident of the Grandin Court section, Durwood Stanley, that Grandin Road was named for a film star, Ethel Grandin. According to Brice's recollection, the legend is that Miss Grandin gave a performance at the old Academy of Music in Roanoke and was so spectacular that one of the developers decided to name a road after her, thus, the naming of Grandin Road. If records exist documenting such an episode, I have not been able to find them. However, Ethel Grandin was indeed a rising film star at that time. Miss Grandin was born in New York City in 1894. Her most famous silent film was Carl Laemmle's *Traffic in Souls* in 1913. Between 1910 and 1922, Miss Grandin starred in over thirty silent films. She ended her screen career when she married and began a family. She died in Woodland Hills, California, in 1988. Again, whether this source of the name of Grandin Road is accurate may never be proven, just as we will never know if Miss Grandin knew of a street in Roanoke being named for her. Given, however, that one of the prominent occupants of Grandin Road is the Grandin Theater, Roanoke's only surviving grand movie house, that the street may have been named for a screen actress makes for a charming and appropriate story.

The success of residential developers generated sufficient interest by the Roanoke Railway and Electric Company that a streetcar line was established into Raleigh Court in 1911, running from the Norwich line on Virginia Avenue west to Grandin Road. The line ran southwest on Grandin, having a terminus near Laburnum Avenue. The streetcar line was double tracked on Grandin Road between Virginia Avenue and Westover in 1923.[18]

A tragedy that struck near the Wasena Bridge on August 23, 1912, made the front page of the next day's *Roanoke Times*. Thomas Gee, a resident of Norwich, was hauling sand from the riverbank when the bank caved in on him. Bearing witness to the event was his twelve-year-old son, Raymond. The newspaper gave the following description of the event:

> *The boy with his father were engaged in hauling sand from a bank in the vicinity of the Wasena bridge near the end of Seventh Avenue, s.w. The bank where Mr. Gee was working was ten or twelve feet high. The veil of sand was about six feet thick and above was a stratum of earth and ashes which had been dumped at that spot. He was digging under the heavy top, and warned by his little son of the danger, but he kept on at work, and suddenly the embankment gave way burying him beneath tons of earth choking and suffocating him, from which he died before he could be extricated.*
>
> *The cries of the boy brought some men from the opposite side of the river, and with willing hands the earth was removed. He was found to be dead. Dr. Simmons, city coroner, was notified, but after viewing the body decided that it was an accident pure and simple and that an inquest was unnecessary. Raymond Gee notified his grandfather, Squire O.L. Gee, and undertaker Peerman was sent for to take charge of the body.*

Gee was twenty-nine years old and was survived by his wife, his son Raymond and a daughter.

In 1913, the Roanoke-Ghent Park Realty Company set aside the land known today as Ghent Hill Park as an amenity to their residential development. The park, located at the western end of Memorial Bridge, had an interesting history over the next few decades. In 1924, park trustees conveyed the land to the city for the express purpose of maintaining it as a park. In 1930, the Central Council PTA asked city leaders to consider renaming the park Adams Memorial Park. The city manager inquired of officials with the Ghent Realty Company, and they opposed the name change. The matter was dropped. In April 1941, city council purchased a belt of land along the Norfolk and Western Railway tracks, from Colonial American National Bank between Wasena Park and Ghent Park, for park purposes. The price was $5,250. In October 1951, Reverend Howard Parker, pastor of the Roanoke Church of Christ, appeared before city council and offered to purchase Ghent Park for $5,000 for purposes of building a church and parsonage thereon. After deliberation, the council was in unanimous agreement not to sell the park, believing the city should be acquiring parklands and not disposing of them.[19]

This area of parkland set aside by the Ghent Realty Company in 1913 was originally called River Bluff Park. On April 5, 1915, the park was officially dedicated with much attention. The *Roanoke Times* reported the dedicatory activities: "The presentation was made by D.W. Persinger, representing the Ghent Realty Company, and the acceptance was made on the part of the citizens by Professor Thomas Phelps, of Virginia Heights, a teacher in Roanoke High School."

According to the newspaper account, Persinger planted a tree, known as the Ghent Tree, in the center of "one of the most commanding knolls in the park." This was followed by remarks from John Wood of Virginia Heights, secretary of the chamber of commerce, who represented the citizens of the neighborhood in expressing appreciation to Ghent Realty. This was followed by comments from Mrs. M.M. Caldwell of the Woman's River Bluff Park Association, who asked her fellow citizens to make "River View one of the most beautiful parks in the section."

After these speeches, neighbors planted more trees in the park that had been donated with the assistance of Boy Scouts and schoolchildren. This day-long planting effort was under the watchful eye of Patrick Foy, a gardener for the Norfolk and Western Railway. "Shrubbery donated by other citizens was planted in a corner of the reservation, near the entrance, and vines were set out on the bluff, overlooking the river. The grounds had been beautifully cleaned and presented an attractive appearance for the opening." Additional beautification plans were announced by Foy as well.

The newspaper concluded,

> *The beauties of the park will afford great pleasure to persons passing on cars and automobiles this summer, as well as much enjoyment to the residents of this section as recreation grounds. Members of the committee in charge of the improvements hope to secure the cooperation of the people in keeping persons from injuring the plants and trees, and the association wishes to serve notice that anyone caught putting or dumping trash on the grounds will be handled by the law.*[20]

The donation of parkland by the Roanoke-Ghent Realty Company in many ways ended that enterprise's presence in the area. A few years earlier, in January 1910, the realty company sold the last of its remaining residential lots. This was not due to individual citizens buying lots and quickly erecting homes, however. It was caused by speculation by other real estate companies as they bought out competitors or added to their holdings. The *Roanoke Times* reported on the transaction in its January 5 edition, "The lots are considered among the most desirable around the city and it is predicted that within the next few years the section will be one of fashionable residences." The newspaper noted the success of the company, saying, "There are perhaps few better pleased holders of Roanoke real estate than those who have invested their money in Ghent. Many lots sold by the company have since changed hands at an advance of 50 to 100 percent. A few bought lots for speculation but a large majority of the lots are held as investments or for improvements. A large number of fine residences will be erected in Ghent during 1910."

The Evergreen Development Company made a significant announcement on October 23, 1915, regarding the purchase of some land within Raleigh Court for the purposes of creating

Memorial Bridge Park adjacent to Ghent Hill Park, circa 1950s. *Courtesy of RPL.*

a new burial park, Evergreen Cemetery. Officers of the company were A.G. Chewning, C.B. Cole and Charles Armes. The company had acquired forty-seven acres, which was a portion of the former Solitude farm that had been purchased several years earlier by the Virginia Heights Corporation.

This announcement for a new cemetery was most welcome to Roanoke's leaders. The City Cemetery was filled, and Fairview was the only other large cemetery near the city. The *Roanoke Times* described the Evergreen Development Company's plans in its October 25 edition:

> *The Evergreen Development Company is capitalized at 100,000 and the plans in contemplation will, when consummated, supply a burial park readily accessible by vehicle and street cars and not too far from the city. The principal feature of the new plan is that from the beginning a substantial portion of the proceeds from the sale of space will be placed in a trust fund, interest from which will insure thorough and perpetual care of all lots. In addition to this attractive feature, the company will devote special attention to beautification and improvement of the land. There will be perfect drainage to begin*

with, and the site is particularly susceptible to beautification at the hands of a landscape engineer. It lies on gentle slopes from north to south that meet in a natural valley not too abruptly but enough to lend to the general parking plans.

The first burial in Evergreen was for Mary Trout in 1916. In its nine decades of existence, Evergreen has had a number of notable burials: fifteen former mayors of the city of Roanoke, one former governor of the commonwealth (Lindsey Almond), a poet laureate of Virginia (Leigh Buckner Hanes), a former ambassador (Carter Burgess), a past president of the Norfolk and Western Railway (R.H. "Racehorse" Smith) and a member of Congress (Posey Lester), among many others.

Also in 1915, the maintenance of the Virginia Avenue Bridge was once again brought before city leaders. The bridge was closed due to poor conditions. Roanoke's Mayor Moomaw, in a letter dated April 5, 1915, reported to the city council that the closing was causing a great inconvenience and that city and county authorities had not been able to agree upon its maintenance. (Remember, at that time one end of the bridge remained in the city and the other in the county.) A study, therefore, had been conducted and, according to Moomaw, 200 feet of the bridge were in the city and 409 feet were in the county. The Virginia Bridge and Iron Company also inspected the bridge to determine the extent of repairs needed. This situation remained unresolved for four years. Finally, in July 1919, the council appealed to the state highway commissioner for assistance. The commissioner worked out an amicable agreement, and repairs to Virginia Avenue Bridge went forward, culminating in its reopening in 1920.

Chapter 2

ANNEXATION AND GROWTH

I n September of 1919, the residents of Raleigh Court were seeking annexation into the city. To assist the citizens in their request, the Roanoke City Council appointed three of its members—R.H. Angell, J.J. Sheehan and E.T. Morris—to serve as the Special Committee on Annexation. On September 20, 1919, that committee made the following report to the council:

> *Your committee appointed to consider the question of annexation of the territory composed of Virginia Heights, Ghent, Wasena, and Raleigh Court, beg me to report that a meeting was held on Thursday, September 18, 1919, at which meeting there was present a committee from the territory proposed to be annexed. After a discussion it was decided that the best interests of the citizens living in the above mentioned territory, as well as the City of Roanoke, would be sub served by annexation. The committee of citizens from the territory proposed to be annexed determined to report to a mass meeting of citizens of such territory a recommendation that such territory be annexed to the City of Roanoke. Your committee prepared a letter setting forth the basis upon which it would agree to annexation…Your committee are [sic] of the opinion that it is highly expedient and essential, if not absolutely necessary, that the territory herein referred to be annexed to the City of Roanoke and it recommends that the proper ordinance be adopted, and that the City Solicitor take immediate steps to perfect such annexation.*

The city council adopted the committee's report and authorized the city manager to begin mapping the territory.[21]

The next day, September 20, a mass meeting of the citizens was convened to receive and respond to the report of the council's annexation committee. J.H. Frantz, chairman of the committee representing the citizens, wrote to Councilman Angell a letter that read as follows:

> *The statement and recommendation contained in your communication of September 19 was duly received and at a mass meeting of the citizens of the proposed annexed territory*

held under the auspices of the Virginia Heights Civic League at the Virginia Heights School building September 20, your communication was submitted for consideration. After careful consideration of statements and proposed recommendations or terms, the following resolution offered by J.C. Martin and seconded by E.W. Speed was declared adopted by counted vote of 63 in favor of its adoption and 4 against its adoption. "Be it resolved that report of the annexation committee of the Virginia Heights Civic League be accepted and the statements and terms outlined in the communication...be and are hereby accepted and that the present committee of this league be continued for the purpose of securing properly signed petitions of the citizens of the proposed annexed territory and render such further assistance as they deem necessary to promote the best interests of the community affected."[22]

Based upon the petitions, the City of Roanoke petitioned the court to annex Raleigh Court. A final ruling was rendered in the city's favor on November 21, 1919, by Judge P.H. Dillard of Rocky Mount after a hearing of several days. Judge Dillard was presiding over the case at the circuit court in Salem in the absence of Judge W.W. Moffett. Essentially, the tracts of Virginia Heights, Raleigh Court, Wasena, Norwich and Ghent were added to the city.

During the annexation hearing, some landowners objected and their land was excluded from the annexation in Judge Dillard's ruling. Those not included were Evergreen Burial Park and the land immediately south of the cemetery, as well as land owned by the Match and Spoke Factories and the Roanoke Lime and Potash Company. One of the main reasons for the exclusion of Evergreen Cemetery was the city's desire at the time that any new cemeteries be located outside the city limits. Further, the attorney for Evergreen asserted that farmland adjoining Evergreen, namely a sixty-nine-acre tract belonging to S.H. Pace and a thirty-acre parcel owned by Miss Mollie Lowman, were only suitable for farming and not any other kind of development. The remaining properties excluded were primarily located on a sixty-acre tract near Norwich.

With Judge Dillard's affirmative ruling, the City of Roanoke acquired territory, embracing about one thousand acres and about five thousand citizens. Additionally, the annexation encompassed properties with an estimated value of $2 million, meaning an increase in annual tax revenue to the city of approximately $36,000. This new tax revenue, however, was to be solely dedicated to improvements in the annexed territory for a period of five years. Annexation also increased the city's political clout in the state legislature. Its representation increased by one more member in the House of Delegates, and the city also became part of a second state senatorial district.[23]

The court set forth certain conditions related to the annexation in deference to Roanoke County. The city would pay the county $17,500 for schoolhouses and equipment, $2,420 as a pro rata share of county indebtedness, $3,520 as a pro rata share of indebtedness of the Big Lick School District, $450 as a pro rata share of the Cave Spring School District's indebtedness and the interest on the outstanding debt just noted.

With annexation now in place and Raleigh Court properly a part of Roanoke City, residential development occurred with more vigor, as builders knew that city services were now guaranteed. As the various land development companies moved forward, restrictions were often put on deeds to ensure proper use of the lots being sold. By contemporary standards, some of the deed restrictions seem peculiar, if not humorous.

A 1921 deed from the Raleigh Court Corporation to a house lot located in the present-day 2200 block of Avenel Avenue contained the following: "No swine shall be kept upon said premises or any part thereof, nor shall the owner or occupant of said premises allow any live stock owned by such owner or occupant to run at large on the premises adjacent to or in the vicinity of said premises hereby conveyed…No intoxicating liquors shall be sold upon said land, or in any of the houses that may be constructed thereon."

In addition to those restrictions, however, came other prohibitions not at all humorous that reflected the rampant bigotry and prejudices of the times. Basically, Raleigh Court was a closed neighborhood to blacks, Jews and certain nationalities. In the same deed just cited was this paragraph: "None of said hereby granted land, nor any portion thereof, shall be hereafter conveyed, sold or leased to any Negro or Syrian, nor shall the same be sold or leased to any Corporation or other person to be used, occupied or leased by any Negro or Syrian." A 1924 deed for property located near Memorial Bridge contained the following language that "said land shall not be sold or rented to negroes or Syrians or their descendants." A 1934 deed for property located near Fishburn Park read, in part, as follows: "No portion of the land shall be sold to be used, owned or occupied by Negroes, Greeks, Assyrians or by any persons who belong to any race or creed or sect which holds, recognizes or observes any day of the week other than the first day of the week to be the Sabbath or his Sabbath, or any corporation or clan composed of or controlled by any such person." Numerous other examples could be cited. The adoption of Jim Crow laws by the Virginia Legislature in 1900 made outright discrimination in housing and other areas legal, and the developers of Raleigh Court took full advantage of the situation.[24]

At the turn of the decade, two businesses in Norwich began operating that would have longtime presences in that section. Harris Hardwood Company opened in 1919. The Walker Machine and Foundry Corporation became established in 1920 with a $100,000 capital stock issue. The foundry worked with iron, aluminum, brass and bronze, and in the mid-1950s employed nearly three hundred workers.

A notable social development within the Virginia Heights community occurred in 1920 when the Virginia Heights Masonic Lodge, No. 324, was organized and began meeting monthly. They met the third Friday of every month in space above Catagoni's Grocery at the corner of Grandin Road and Virginia (Memorial) Avenue, according to their listing in the 1921 city directory.

With annexation, municipal investment began to occur to serve the new citizens. On February 26, 1921, the Roanoke School Board presented a request to the city council for a four-room schoolhouse to be constructed in Norwich. A month later, the board informed council that the cost would be approximately $20,000, plus acquisition of the site. In

Virginia Heights Elementary School, 1922. *Courtesy of HSWV.*

May, the council authorized the expenditure of $1,565 for the purchase of the Norwich School site, and the next month the school was under construction. The contractor was Martin Brothers. Norwich School officially opened the first day of the 1921–22 school year on September 7. The *Roanoke Times* reported, "The long felt need of additional school facilities in Norwich has been supplied, the new school building having been completed for a cost of nearly $20,000…The new building, situated on the Norwich car line and conveniently located for the inhabitants of that section, has four large rooms, well lighted and heated." An estimated 115 pupils enrolled at Norwich School in September 1921.

The Norwich School was linked to Virginia Heights Elementary School in that the principal at Virginia Heights also oversaw the Norwich School. For most of its existence, the Norwich facility would house the lower grades, with the students then moving to Virginia Heights for the upper grades. The teachers at Norwich during its inaugural year were Miss Mary Hinton, Miss Claudine Avent and Mrs. Myrtle Weeks. Miss Mable Massey served as principal to both schools.[25]

While the school board was lobbying council for funds for Norwich, it was also looking to expand Virginia Heights School. The original 1906 structure was no longer accommodating the section's growing enrollment. The board had requested $34,000 to erect an eight-room addition. Council concurred, and construction on the addition commenced in 1922. Midway through the 1922–23 school year, the addition was put to use. For the opening of the 1923–24 session, the new building became occupied for the first time for a full academic year. There was little fanfare over the new structure. The *Roanoke Times*, on September 12, gave it a brief mention in a lengthy article about the start of the school year. "One new school building—Virginia Heights—will be in use this term and will materially relieve the congestion that exists in that section." With the addition, land at the school was consumed, leaving little area for outdoor recreation by the students. Consequently, in February 1924 the city purchased five adjoining lots from Mrs. Hickey and Dr. George Lawson to expand the school. The purchase of the lots totaled $9,500.

In the summer of 1921, city council was making plans for a fire station to service the newly annexed area. The present-day site of the fire station on Memorial Avenue was acquired by the city for $4,160 in late June. Frye and Stone Architects were contracted to design the station, and on May 27, 1922, Martin Brothers was awarded the bid to erect the facility at a cost of $17,450. (A second bay was added to the original portion of the station in 1950.) The station, to be known as No. 7, was opened on December 13 of that year. A new engine was purchased for the station, a "750-gallon pump, hose and chemical wagon." Six positions were added to the fire department to man the new station, and the original crew was led by Captain J.T. Allman, formerly the captain of No. 3 Company.[26]

With various improvements now occurring within the area, real estate developers stepped up their efforts to promote residential growth. The Raleigh Court

Fire Station No. 7 in 1929. Note the Jamison's store sign on the grocery building in the background. *Courtesy of SHS.*

Corporation placed a large advertisement in a November 1924 edition of the *Roanoke Times* that read as follows:

> *A large number of homes are being built in Raleigh Court and many more are planned for early spring. Lots in our fine new section east of Grandin Road and north of the Methodist church are rapidly being selected since the financial condition of the country has become more settled. It has inspired our progressive people to begin building and planning new homes more vigorous than they did a year ago before the slump. A quick return to prosperous business has taught Roanoke people to realize that slight depressions in business cannot stop the growth and development of our beautiful city. Owning houses and lots in Roanoke City is different from owning them in a sleepy and unprogressive town.*

It should be noted that the "dividing line" between Virginia Heights and Raleigh Court was Windsor Avenue at its intersection with Grandin Road. In fact, for many years large stone columns stood on opposite corners of Windsor, having been erected by the Raleigh Court Corporation to mark the entrance into their new section.

Before and during the 1920s, many prominent Roanokers moved to Raleigh Court, erecting grand homes along Virginia (Memorial) Avenue and Grandin Road. In 1908, real estate developer Manley Caldwell, a Wytheville native, built Walker Hall. Caldwell's residence (1525 Memorial) contained a temple-style portico and Ionic columns. At this same time, M.A. Riffe, president of the Virginia Heights Corporation, constructed a Queen Anne–style home with turret, gables and a wraparound porch with Corinthian classical columns (1601 Memorial).

Avon Road, 1929. *Courtesy of SHS.*

Along Grandin Road, C.E. Michaels, president of the Virginia Bridge and Iron Company, constructed a large Colonial Revival residence in 1913. The home (1731 Grandin) originally was on the corner of Grandin and Sherwood and was moved over one lot in the 1950s to accommodate the construction of the Grandin Road post office. Michaels later constructed the house at 2231 Grandin, after selling his original home to Claude Dudley, president of the Norwich Supply Company.

The Ring House (1802 Grandin) was built in 1925 for M.F. Ring, president of Roanoke City Mills. It is an outstanding example of the Spanish Colonial Revival–style architecture.

Real estate developer Robert Shafer built a Tudor-style home in 1914 (1856 Grandin), and across the street (1857 Grandin) E.H. Johnson, president of Virginia Supply Company, erected a Colonial Revival–style home with Federal detailing. This fine residence was built in 1916. It was later sold to Robert H. Angell, founder of the Shenandoah Life Insurance Company.

In the next block of Grandin Road, other prominent Roanokers continued building large homes. E.H. Ould, president of First National Exchange Bank, built an Italian Renaissance dwelling (1902 Grandin) in 1930. The Tudor Revival–style home at 1920 Grandin Road was built in 1925 for real estate developer S. Duerson. Morton Turner, the first president of American National Bank, erected the Colonial Revival home at 1930 Grandin in 1928. Thus, by the close of the 1920s, bank presidents, real estate developers and business leaders were lending to Raleigh Court a certain aristocratic prominence and prestige with their regal residences.

Apartment house on Windsor Avenue, 1929. *Courtesy of SHS.*

In 1924, one of the most ambitious plans for the Raleigh Court area was announced by the Kazim Temple. What residents of Raleigh Court call Shrine Hill came into being when the Shriners voted to buy a tract of land encompassing the present-day site of Patrick Henry High School. The 101-acre tract was purchased for $237,500 for the following purposes: to erect a mosque for the Shrine, which would contain an auditorium of 3,000 seating capacity, reading rooms, quarters for officers, clubhouse and other departments; to construct a modern stadium of concrete, seating between 25,000 and 30,000; to open a nine-hole golf course, with hopes of adding another nine holes at a future date; to put in tennis courts; and to build a swimming pool. This mammoth undertaking had been four years in the making and was approved by the Roanoke-area Shriners at their meeting on November 8 by a vote of 500 to 3. Earlier, on August 29, a special committee had been formed to develop the project for presentation. Members of that committee included C.B. Wilson, C.M. Armes, J.O.D. Copenhaver, R. Lee Lynn and E.R. Johnson.

The committee had presented the Shriners with a well-developed plan. First, the project was to be located "at the end of the Raleigh Court car line on Grandin Road, left side, owned by the Gordon Heights Corporation" with the purchase price previously stated. Second, a mosque was to be constructed for an estimated $550,000. Surrounding the structure would be Kazim Park, with a clubhouse, recreation field and stadium. Third, the location had been chosen because "it is located in the fastest growing section of the city, accessible from every part over main thoroughfares, on a street car line, and has a commanding topography."

The committee had retained the services of landscape architect Sid J. Hare to design the park and grounds. Hare further commented in his own written assessment of the tract as follows:

Intersection of Shirley Avenue and Greenwood Road, circa 1920s. *Courtesy of HSWV.*

The ground is ideally located and decidedly suited for all the purposes spoken of…As for the Shrine site at the top of the hill, I feel that all who visit the building would always remember the vistas and views to the mountains and hills and to the city. From this site one would also view the players on the grounds, the children to the east of the building and your members who play golf who will use the remaining ground as a golf course, would be both in full view of the Temple building.

A finance committee, composed of W.G. Baldwin, W.L. Andrews, Lawrence S. Davis, A.G. Chewning, J.P. Saul Jr. and Dr. S.S. Gale, concurred with the building committee's recommended plan, adding that "according to the present financial statement of the Kazim Temple, there is no question in our mind but what this tract can be purchased and paid for by the Temple."

Following the nearly unanimous vote of the Shriners in attendance at the November 8 meeting to proceed with the land purchase and project, C.B. Wilson of the building committee declared, "This is one of the greatest civic enterprises ever planned for Roanoke." Wilson explained that for four years this "playground of the Masonry" would, with its mosque, house the Shriners in "regal style." Wilson shared that an architect had not yet been retained and that the plans adopted were preliminary, but the fundraising for the project would move forward quickly.

After the business session and adoption of the building committee's report, approximately 2,500 Nobles and their ladies attended an elaborate Potentate's Ball at the City Auditorium, concluding what must have been an energetic and productive fall meeting.[27]

Within a few months, the Shriners launched their fundraising campaign. "1,500 Shriners to Invade City" read a front page headline in the *Roanoke Times* on May 16, 1925. "Probably fifteen hundred Shriners will be in attendance at Kazim Temple's spring ceremonial here today to be staged under a tent which has been pitched in the 'Garden of Allah,' the one hundred acre tract of land acquired recently by the Shrine just of Grandin Road to Raleigh Court. Indications point to the biggest celebration ever staged by Kazim Temple here."[28]

The next day, Shriners crowded into the tent for the Garden of Allah ceremonial in Raleigh Court. "After a short business session at the Masonic Temple, the Shriners wended their way to the future 'Garden of Allah' off Grandin Road, where they found a huge tent erected upon a knoll in the center of the property and upon the very spot that the proposed mosque is to occupy. One look at the magnificent view afforded from this point and the majority of the visiting Nobles were converted into enthusiastic supporters of the undertaking," reported the *Times*. Within forty-eight hours, the Shriners launched the campaign to raise $400,000 among its membership for their proposed mosque. An architectural rendering of the grand structure ran in the newspaper, with the campaign literature describing the knoll in Raleigh Court as "the most beautiful spot in America." To be surrounded by the professionally designed Garden of Allah, the mosque and its environs would become "unexcelled in beauty in this section." The mosque was described as being of "handsome proportions, of the ancient architectural style employed by the Moors, unique, majestic, and entrancing." The first-floor entrance would lead to an open-air terrace on either side, overlooking the expansive grounds. The first floor would contain a large lounge, along with a large banquet hall, dining room, private dining rooms and administrative offices. The second floor would be occupied by an immense auditorium with a stage, dressing rooms and property rooms. This same floor would be complemented by reading and writing rooms, game rooms, private rooms and lodge rooms. The ground floor would be reserved for recreational purposes. A detached guesthouse would contain thirty-three rooms to accommodate overnight visitors.

The drive for $400,000 was well organized. The campaign united the entire jurisdiction from Lynchburg to Appalachia, involving some three hundred Nobles. The territory of the Kazim Temple was divided into fifteen zones, under the direction of Noble J.O.D. Copenhaver. The zones were as follows: Lynchburg, Lexington, Roanoke (led by J.A. Turner), Martinsville, Christiansburg, Pulaski, Galax, Wytheville, Tazewell, Marion, Richlands, Bristol, Dante, Norton and Appalachia. The goal of the effort was to solicit each member of the Kazim to make a loan to the Kazim Temple Corporation without interest. On complete payment of each loan, there would be issued a certificate of indebtedness. The amount of the loan was to be paid to the estate or beneficiary of the loaner at his death, or to the loaner himself in case of disability. This arrangement worked to some degree like life insurance money. Loans would be received from the minimum of $200 and up. "The plan has been received with great favor and success in building Temples in other communities and will undoubtedly find a loyal response in behalf of this great movement of Kazim Temple to secure a permanent home. Every Noble will be asked to be a Temple builder and their names will be entered in the cornerstone of the mosque and in a permanent record to be kept in the mosque." [29] With this, the campaign was launched.

For the next several days the *Roanoke Times* kept its readers updated as to the Shriners' progress. "Kazim Temple Begins Drive, Zone 13 Over the Top" read a headline dated May 19. Campaign workers dined together at 6:30 every night of that week to report their progress. Members were reporting donations from as far away as New York City and Miami, Florida. Congressman Clifton A. Woodrum was heavily involved, showing up at various campaign dinner meetings throughout the temple's region and giving motivational speeches. "Shriners Pass $100,000 Mark, Two Zones Are Over Top" ran the headline of May 20. State Senator R.O. Crockett of Tazewell was working in southwestern Virginia with much success, as Galax was leading in pledged loans after two days. A few days later, the *Roanoke Times* proclaimed, "Enthusiasm in Kazim Temple's Drive for Mosque Is Growing." By day three of the campaign, pledged loans totaled $158,750. Securing loans from Roanoke City Shriners were H.T. Martin, Cecil E. Bertie, H.B. Gray, J.W.J. Goff, S.R. Mason, John Antrim, W.F. Davis and F.B. Reid.

On May 27, after the announced eight days of the campaign ended, the Shriners were short by nearly $57,000. Needing the full amount, Shrine leaders nevertheless declared the campaign a success and committed to a quiet campaign in sections distant from Roanoke. Some 1,200 Nobles in the territory solicited had not pledged, and campaign leaders believed their late commitments would put the campaign over the top. Of all the Nobles, 1,502 had made pledged loans, with the average loan being $229. Roanoke's Shriners had pledged over $192,000. [30] Though the amount pledged was significant, it fell short of the goal and the Shriners ultimately abandoned the project.

While Shriners were planning a grand complex in the Shrine Hill area, local Masons announced plans for a lodge in Virginia Heights along Grandin Road. On December 20, 1924, members of the Virginia Heights Lodge, who were meeting at the time above a grocery store, publicly put forward their intention to construct a two-story brick temple, estimated to cost $40,000, at 112 Grandin Road. The *Roanoke World News* reported,

> *Work on the new building will commence this spring, it was declared, and it is planned to use the basement for banquet purposes. It will be equipped with a kitchenette and other conveniences. On the ground floor will be two store rooms and the top floor will be used as a lodge room. This lodge was opened four years ago with a membership of seventy-five. It is in a prosperous condition and there are now three hundred and eighteen members.*

Dairy Fountain at the intersection of Carter Road and Brandon Avenue under construction in 1929. *Courtesy of SHS.*

At the same annual meeting where the lodge plans were approved and announced, the following officers were elected: F.W. Kling, worshipful master; S.R. Truman, senior warden; H.I. Coiner, junior warden; L.R. Tucker, treasurer; Oscar Graves, secretary; J.V. Barnes, senior deacon; and H.L. Merricks Jr., junior deacon.[31]

With the ongoing commercial and residential development of Raleigh Court, city infrastructure needed to be improved. Notably, the bridge over the Roanoke River at Thirteenth Street—the Virginia Avenue Bridge (also known as Woodrum Bridge)—was no longer adequately serving the transportation needs for accessing Raleigh Court. In 1924, Roanoke voters approved a bond issue that financed what would become Memorial Bridge.

The naming of the bridge was marred by controversy. Following the end of World War I, the city council had tried to determine a suitable memorial for those who had served in the war. One suggestion was a marker in Elmwood Park. Ultimately, the council adopted a resolution on December 8, 1925, to name the new bridge "Memorial Bridge." Local veterans groups, however, were dissatisfied, believing the naming of the bridge was not necessary. In short, the veterans decided to boycott the bridge's dedication.

Memorial Bridge opened to traffic on May 6, 1926, but was not officially dedicated until August 30. Memorial Bridge is 54 feet wide and 785 feet long and was constructed at a cost of $282,750 (the original cost estimate was $258,000). Consisting of five 120-foot spans, the bridge was built by W.W. Boxley in about eleven months. Boxley, along with James and Norma Towles, inaugurated the bridge by riding the first vehicle across

Memorial Bridge under construction, with Virginia Avenue Bridge on left. *Courtesy of RPL.*

the structure. (It should be noted that Walnut Avenue and Jefferson Street bridges were also funded and built about this time.)

At the dedication ceremony, speakers included Congressman Clifton A. Woodrum, Judge Robert C. Jackson and Councilman Charles Fox. Music for the ceremony was furnished by the Dokkie Band, and Dr. Richard Owens, pastor of Calvary Baptist Church, delivered the invocation. Mayor Blair Fishburn officiated the ceremony. According to the *Roanoke Times*, "Congressman Woodrum delivered an eloquent oration setting forth the high principles on which America has always gone to war, and lauded the spirit of her fighting men who have sacrificed all in perpetuating their country's freedom." Judge Jackson deemed the bridge a wise expenditure of tax dollars and complimented its "incomparable beauty." Councilman Fox dedicated the structure and unveiled the bronze plaques.

Before several hundred spectators, Boy Scouts assisted with the unveiling of the four large bronze plaques. The city council had decided upon the quotations, using the words of Patrick Henry, Theodore Roosevelt, Thomas "Stonewall" Jackson and Thomas Jefferson. Following the unveilings, the crowd was led in singing the chorus "America."

To complete the history of Memorial Bridge, the structure was rededicated on Veterans Day, (November 11) 1991, following needed restoration. In April 2002, a complete restoration of the bridge was initiated, removing old embedded streetcar track, reinforcing the concrete and patching asphalt for a total cost of $1.4 million. Interestingly, one of the persons in the crowd at the 1991 rededication was Richard Pence, a retired attorney who was one of the Boy Scouts who had participated in the original dedication service of 1926.[32]

One of the early controversies to engage the Raleigh Court residents during their first decade of being in the city was the proposal in April 1925 to place a detention house at the southern terminus of the Thirteenth Street Bridge, just before the Memorial Bridge. On April 7, neighborhood leaders met in the Masonic Lodge hall on Grandin Road to discuss the situation. City Manager William Hunter brought prepared remarks on the proposal, which was met with stiff opposition. Neighborhood leaders were concerned about the proposed project's impact upon the residential quality of their section, but there were also racial prejudices involved. The *Roanoke Times* reported, "One of the chief objections was a contention that the detention house would have both white and colored people and that it would amount to bringing colored residents into a section where they are not given the right to reside." The result of the night's gathering was to appoint a committee to represent neighborhood concerns before the next meeting of city council. J.H. Frantz, S.R. Truman and H.P. Glasgow were selected to fulfill the obligation. Additionally, Oscar Graves, C.C. Nelms and W.H. Coleman were charged with organizing a citizens' meeting the following week to continue the discussion.

On April 14, a crowd estimated to exceed two hundred residents attended a follow-up meeting at the Masonic hall. Former State Senator W.D. Andrews opened the meeting. After several speakers were heard, the residents were in unanimous agreement to oppose the plan. The group adopted a formal resolution for presentation to the city council. Reasons cited in the resolution for opposing the home were "the creation of

Memorial Bridge dedication ceremony, 1925. *Courtesy of HSWV.*

Memorial Bridge dedication ceremony, 1925. *Courtesy of HSWV.*

Memorial Bridge, circa 1930. *Courtesy of HSWV.*

an eyesore to people of one of the fairest residential sections of our city," "detriment to property values," "one of the worst advertisements to visitors and tourists along the Lee Highway," "detrimental to the health of the unfortunate children who would be therein confined and a continuing humiliation to them and their friends." Interestingly, nothing was recorded relating to the racial issues that had apparently been so evident at the first meeting. The residents suggested, therefore, that the detention home be located on the city farm property (where present-day Virginia Western Community College is located).

On April 24, the citizens of Raleigh Court appeared before the council with petitions and representative speakers. Joining with the opposition were some fifty physicians within the valley, the Real Estate Board, the men's Bible class of Raleigh Court Methodist Church, Judge W.V. Henson and the Virginia Heights School PTA. The council, upon a motion offered by Mayor J.B. Fishburn, decided to abandon the proposed site and refer the matter back to the Welfare Board for further investigation as to other, more appropriate sites.[33]

In the summer of 1925, citizens residing in the subdivisions of Grandin Court, Weaver Heights and Lee-Hy Court began to organize in support of being annexed into the city. On August 14, Mr. M.F. Weaver presented a petition asking that the city take steps to have Weaver Heights Addition annexed. He stated that there were eighty-five houses in the addition and that all except one or two had signed the petition for annexation. Councilman Charles Fox moved to have the territory annexed following a completed survey of the area by the city manager. Fox's motion passed unanimously. The following month, on September 8, City Manager William Hunter reported back to the council with a completed survey and city council adopted a formal resolution authorizing the city manager to petition the court to annex Weaver Heights, Grandin Court and Lee-Hy Court. In addition to these residential areas, Evergreen Burial Park, whose lands had been excluded during the 1919 annexation, became a part of the annexed territory.[34]

The court ruled in late December in favor of the city's petition and the southwest perimeter of the city expanded. The lands officially became a part of the city on January 1, 1926. In addition to the areas just discussed, the city also annexed at this same time Villa Heights, Rugby and Morningside. As part of the annexation, there were terms similar to those imposed during the 1919 annexation. The city paid Roanoke County $9,000 as a pro rata share of the Big Lick School District's indebtedness, $1,200 as a pro rata share of the Cave Spring School District's indebtedness, the interest on the combined pro rata debt of those two districts and $150 for a pro rata share of the county's indebtedness on bonds. Further, all taxes collected from the newly annexed citizens had to be directly reinvested into the annexed territory for the next five years.

The development of the Weaver Heights subdivision had been spearheaded by T.R. Tillett and W.C. Weaver. Tillett, a native of Loudon County, had come to Roanoke in 1890, where he had been elected city sergeant (police chief) in 1894. He died just a few months after his development became annexed, at age sixty-nine, on May 17, 1927. Weaver succumbed to the fragile economic realities of 1930. He filed for bankruptcy on December 4 of that year, noting liabilities of $408,000 and assets of $206,000, and thus faded from Roanoke's business landscape.[35]

In April 1927, residents benefited from the opening of their first neighborhood library. The City of Roanoke opened the Virginia Heights Library Station in the Masonic Lodge building on Grandin Road. The station recorded for that initial year 404 registered borrowers who could select from a collection of 1,184 volumes. The library would remain in the Masonic Lodge for the next five years.

On July 12, 1927, the voters of Roanoke approved a bond referendum that incorporated a request from the Roanoke School Board to spend $750,000 for the purpose of new school buildings, lands and additions. This was significant for Raleigh Court, as it created the capacity to erect two new schools: Wasena Elementary and Woodrow Wilson Junior High.

Wasena Elementary School opened its classroom doors on Monday morning, October 9, 1928. Two hundred students walked through them. The new building had seven rooms for regular classes, first through sixth grades, and another room for a "sight-saving" class. School officials reported after the first day that everything was "moving smoothly and in perfect order."

On opening day, the Wasena faculty consisted of Miss Emma Smith, principal; Nelf Walters, Bessie Ragland, Laura Johnson, Anna Cooper, Pearl Pittard and Helen Birkenmeyer, regular classroom teachers; and Mrs. Katherine Cook Huffman, sight-

Aerial view of Memorial Bridge, 1928. *Courtesy of SHS.*

Wasena Elementary School, circa 1930. *Courtesy of HSWV.*

saving class teacher. Miss Smith had served previously as the assistant principal at the Commerce Street School downtown. Prior to their new assignments at Wasena, the faculty had been serving at Park, West End and Virginia Heights Schools. The *Roanoke Times* complimented the facility by proclaiming it "one of the most beautifully fitted units in the local system."[36]

Woodrow Wilson Junior High School had experienced construction delays during that summer and was late to open. Students entered their new school on Tuesday, October 24, 1928. An estimated 375 students enrolled there the first day. The new junior high school contained fourteen classrooms, two rooms combined for an assembly hall, a principal's office, a library and a teachers' workroom, all complemented by a 17-member faculty. That year was a significant one for the Roanoke School System. In addition to the two new schools in Raleigh Court, the school board had also constructed an annex for Jackson Junior High, along with three other new school buildings: Morningside Elementary, Forest Park Elementary and Lucy Addison High School. This surge in new construction was warranted, however, in that the previous school year some 3,000 students had been placed on a part-time class schedule due to lack of facilities. With this new construction, that number had been reduced to 300 for the 1928–29 academic year.[37]

With the new Woodrow Wilson Junior High School, across Carter Road from the school there was a triangle area of land really not suitable for a residence. This "triangular park" was purchased by the city from Joseph Angell in May 1929 for $2,250. Several months later, on November 1, a group of Woodrow Wilson students appeared before city council and presented a resolution asking that the small triangle be named Woodrow Wilson Plot. The students who spoke at the meeting were Neville Ammen, Edward Dowdy, Elizabeth Mountcastle and Charles Steele. The matter was laid over. Given the small amount of land involved, the matter seemed to consume an inordinate amount of the council's attention. A few weeks later, a second petition was submitted to council requesting that they, not the students, determine a name for the property. The issue last appears in the council minutes on July 31, 1931, when a committee consisting of Mrs. John Wright, Mrs. D.R. Hunt, Mrs. T.J. Hughes and Mrs. C.A. Kastendike, representing the executive board of the Roanoke City Woman's Club, withdrew their request to name the small plot and requested that the matter be turned over to the Parent-Teacher Association of Woodrow Wilson for them to be given permission to name and beautify the plot. Council adopted that recommendation and asked the PTA to coordinate their efforts with the city manager. If a name was ever designated, it is not recorded.[38]

In the fall of 1927, the Greater Raleigh Court area became better connected to other residential sections when Brandon Avenue was extended from its intersection at Main Street to Franklin Road. A bit of history regarding Brandon Avenue (originally called Brandon Road) is in order. Brandon was originally laid out by the Virginia Heights Extension Company in 1916 in its desire to create another point of access into that section. At that time, Brandon ran from Grandin Road to Main Street. The original intersection of Brandon and Main was not well planned and the topography created a twelve-foot drop outside the curve that linked the two roads. In 1926, this steep curve, wrongly angled, was the site of a single-car accident that took two lives when the auto plunged over the embankment. In that same year, City Manager W.P. Hunter approached H.C. Barnes about donating a right of way through his property from the Main-Brandon intersection to Murray Run. With Barnes in agreement, Hunter then acquired a right of way from Murray Run to Franklin Road, making the connection complete. Brandon was finished as a hard-surface road to Franklin Road in late 1927, becoming one of the most traveled thoroughfares at that time.[39]

On June 6, 1931, the Roanoke Library Board made the decision to proceed with creating a building to house the Virginia Heights Branch. That building would be the Tudor-style structure, now owned by the Greater Raleigh Court Civic League, which sits in the 1900 block of Memorial Avenue today. The building was to be erected by M.J. Patsel for a cost of about $10,000 with a five-year lease for library purposes. This new location would supplant the library's quarters in the Masonic Temple. The library board estimated that the new building would be able to accommodate between five and six thousand volumes. The architectural firm of Eubank and Caldwell designed the building so that half of it could be partitioned, should the library not need the full space.[40] Ground broke for the new branch library by the end of the month. The new branch facility opened that September. The city would buy the building in 1941 for $9,000, ending the lease arrangement. The library would be at this location for the next thirty-four years.

Readers of the *Roanoke Times* were introduced to "Roanoke's New Theater" in the Sunday, November 1, 1931 edition. There, on an inside page, was an artist's sketch of what would become the Grandin Theater. The smartly drawn rendering contained a caption of basic information. "The new structure will be modern in every respect and will cost approximately $100,000. The theater will have a seating capacity of 1,000 and will be equipped with a beautifully designed mezzanine and lounges. The building will be especially constructed for the showing of sound pictures, contracts for which have already been signed." The theater was a project of the Community Theater Corporation, whose offices were located on the fifth floor of the Boxley Building downtown. At the time of the announced plans, no name had been selected for the theater, so the officers of the corporation held a contest and received submissions for the next thirty days. Officers of the corporation were M. Lindsey, president; M.J. Patsel and J.D. Turner, vice-presidents; and Nick Walters, secretary-treasurer.

Within a few months, as the theater was nearing completion, the Junior Woman's Club decided to sponsor the theater's opening night, slated for March 26. The club used the event as a means to raise funds for its school for crippled children, located at 1501 Pattteson Avenue. Miss Clara Black was named chairman of the ticket committee, and was assisted by Mrs. J.H. Lawrence, Mrs. Cutchin Hodges and Mrs. H.L. Gardner.[41]

Raleigh Court Branch Library, circa 1930s. *Courtesy of HSWV.*

In the following months, more details of the theater's construction were reported.

The theater was especially constructed with attention to sound effects and is declared to provide unusually good results in all parts of the building. A modern high-low intensity projector makes objects on the screen distinct from any angle on the main floor or gallery and removes the glare from the front of the screen…Ceiling lighting, arranged in blue and amber, is diffused from three owl reflectors on each side of the auditorium. A star-light effect is provided at each of the two balconies at the front of the theater, while the various shades and blended effects produced from the stage footlights add greatly to the beauty of the interior. The ceiling, accentuated by the lighting arrangements, is especially striking, carrying out in delicate decorative effects the Spanish theme.

All this design was under the watchful eye of Eubank and Caldwell architectural firm. Former Roanoker John R. Brophy was brought back to manage the theater, as he had worked in the film industry for twelve years in New York and on the West Coast.

As opening night drew closer, the Junior Woman's Club was in high gear. The opening for that Saturday night was to begin at 8:15 with the feature film *Arrowsmith*, starring Roland Colman and Helen Hayes. To help promote the opening, the women organized a parade the weekend prior, with a police escort and headed by Mayor S.P. Seifert and City Manager W.P. Hunter. The automobile parade snaked its way through downtown with banners on every car announcing ticket sales for the benefit of the club's school. The goal was nothing less than a sellout of the thousand-seat theater. Thurman and Boone Furniture store also made tickets available through their cashiers. On the day of opening night, ticket-bearing club members stationed themselves in the lobbies of hotels throughout the city in an effort to attract those visiting from out of town. The morning paper of March 26 reported, "Tests at the theater were completed yesterday afternoon and everything declared in readiness for the show tonight. Dancers and musicians also conducted a rehearsal last night and acclimated themselves for their performances."

At 7:00 p.m. on Saturday, March 26, the doors to the Grandin Theater officially opened. Last-minute ticket buyers lined up at the box office window, while Junior Woman's Club members ushered patrons to their seats. At 8:15, the curtain was pulled back and the gala commenced. The *Roanoke Times* covered the evening in great detail:

> *Arrowsmith, starring Ronald Colman and Helen Hayes, was the initial number on the program. The story of the picture deals with the struggle of Martin Arrowsmith, young medical student from the Middle West, in attaining his ambition of becoming a research scientist, an attainment which costs him many of his most cherished friends and ideals.*
>
> *Sea Legs, a musical revue, and Shipwrecked, a "looney tune" cartoon, offered dramatic relief and set the stage for the dancing troupe.*
>
> *Beautiful costumes, enhanced by striking lighting effects produced with the blending of shades from the footlights, made the dance numbers unusually attractive. This entire portion of the program, from opening chorus, soft shoe dance, syncopated tap dance, to a very individual number by Miss Martha Turner and Hubert Smith and the concluding appearance of the ensemble received continued applause.*
>
> *The dance numbers follow: Opening chorus—Miss Eloise Rhodes, Miss Augusta Grove, Miss Jane White, Miss Hattie Beck, Miss Mildred Crewes, Miss Florence Spindle, Mrs. John Redd, and Mrs. Eugene Gibson.*
>
> *Soft Shoe Dance—Misses Floyd and Dorothea Ward.*
>
> *Syncopated tap dance—Miss Betsy Smith, Miss Mary Pendleton Smythe, Miss Pheobe McClaugherty, Miss Jane Phenix, Miss Frederica Swann, Misses Floyd and Dorothea Ward, and Mrs. James Swartzel.*
>
> *Miss Martha Turner and Hubert Smith, Miss Mavia Taylor served as accompanists.*
>
> *"First Nighters" were greeted by eight members of the club who served as ushers for the evening. They are: Miss May Bierley, Mrs. Juball Angell, Mrs. Ruth Jackson, Miss Kizzie Burnette, Mrs. Ina Hodges, Miss Azile Wade, Miss Mary Wirsing and Miss Thelma Dixon.*

The leaders of the Junior Woman's Club—namely Miss Essie Dyer, president, and Miss Clara Black, event chairman—pronounced the three-hour gala a success. The event was attended by over eight hundred persons and helped the Woman's Club retire a $1,600 debt on their school for disabled children. More importantly to Raleigh Court, however, was the opening of the Grandin Theater, which is now Roanoke's only remaining historic theater.[42]

On January 19, 1934, Roanoke City Council officially noted the gift by Junius B. Fishburn of real estate that created Wasena Park. The twenty-eight-acre tract was offered to the city by Fishburn to be used for "park and recreation" purposes. Council immediately requested that the city manager develop a plan for the area, and landscape architect A.A. Farnham was hired. Farnham developed a park with both natural and recreational amenities that was favored by both the council and Fishburn. This would be the first of three tracts that Fishburn would deed to the city, resulting in parks (Wasena, Norwich and Lakewood) for the Greater Raleigh Court area.

Residents of Raleigh Court stood along Virginia Avenue and Grandin Road on October 19, 1934, and watched the motorcade of President Franklin Roosevelt slowly wind its way through their environs en route to the dedication of the Veterans Administration Hospital in Salem. The processional came through Raleigh Court as Congressman Clifton Woodrum's mother, a resident of Thirteenth Street, wished to speak briefly to the president. Judge James Brice, who was a young boy at the time, remembers standing on the curb along Grandin Road with many others waving small American flags as the president's car passed by. Flanking the president that day in the car were Congressman Woodrum and Roanoke's mayor, Sidney Small.

In 1936, the Coffee Pot and its adjacent filling station opened on Brambleton Avenue. Originally designed as a teahouse for roadside travelers, the restaurant was later named to the National Register of Historic Places in 1996.

Raleigh Court Park came into existence in 1936. On August 28, city council took action to acquire the land adjoining Woodrow Wilson Junior High School, approximately 9.02 acres, by authorizing the purchase of the land from the West Raleigh Court Land Company for $15,000. In the City's Comprehensive Plan of 1928 (the Nolen Plan), the property is identified as "Sherwood Park," probably a designation given to it by the private land development company as it was bounded by Sherwood Avenue. As has been previously noted, the land development companies often set aside park areas that were either acquired later by the city for municipal use or developed by the private sector.

For many years, the residents of Virginia Heights had been petitioning for improved mail service. Back in October 1915, for example, the Virginia Heights Civic League had organized a petition drive to request city mail service into the section. Virginia Heights had been, prior to annexation, a rural, free delivery route. In 1937, the postal service opened the Virginia Heights substation in Clore's Drugstore at 128 Grandin Road (the 1300 block today). Philip Clore, the proprietor, was appointed as the acting postal clerk.[43]

Lakewood Pond, circa 1920s. *Courtesy of HSWV.*

In 1937, another major park was added to the Raleigh Court neighborhood. For many years the city had been using land, known as Lakewood, along Brandon Avenue for park purposes. Though the land was privately owned, the city had agreed to maintain the land for park purposes in exchange for public use of it. In fact, in July 1928, E.C. Johnson and H.L. Lawson, representing the Lakewood Corporation, had appeared before the city council and presented a proposition to sell the Lakewood parkland, about fifteen acres, to the city for $40,000. The council considered the proposal but ultimately declined on the basis of budgetary constraints. Nonetheless, the city and Lakewood Corporation did work out an arrangement for land to serve as a public park. In 1937, Junius B. Fishburn engaged Mayor Sidney Small in a series of conversations about donating the land for a municipal park. On November 20, Fishburn wrote a letter to the mayor formally proposing the gift and extending a challenge to the council.

> *I have always been tremendously interested in the development of a considerably better park system in Roanoke. I still think Roanoke is lagging far behind in the development of public parks and recreational facilities, and I hope very much that the city will not only receive other gifts for park purposes, but will also buy additional land for park development as rapidly as possible while park sites are still available.*

On November 22, city council voted unanimously to receive the land, and the following week the council acted to name the area "Lakewood Park." Seven years later, in June 1944, J.P. Fishburn donated an additional three acres along present-day Brambleton Avenue, which expanded the park in size.[44]

By the late 1930s, Wasena residents were advocating for a new bridge into their neighborhood that would connect Elm Avenue to Main Street. For many years, an old steel bridge had served that purpose, but it was no longer able to accommodate increasing traffic loads.

The original Wasena Bridge had been erected in 1912 by the Wasena Land Company. The steel bridge erected by the land company was near the location of an old ore railroad bridge. This narrow-gauge railroad bridge had served as a link to the Rorer iron ore mines lying south of present-day Peakwood Drive. Though the little railroad that served the mines was abandoned in the 1890s, the little steel bridge was still maintained and used as a means of traversing the Roanoke River, at least until the arrival of the Wasena Land Company. With the developers came a desire to abandon the railroad bridge and erect a new steel bridge, which they did. This bridge opened Wasena to development and served the area for many years. At the time the bridge was built, there were few automobiles and streetcars were much shorter and lighter. The bridge had been repaired numerous times, but finally the city had to post signs at each end warning that traffic crossed at its own peril. (One interesting side note on the bridge and automobiles was a complaint received by the city manager in 1920 that autos were speeding across the bridge dangerously. The manager agreed and put the posted speed limit on the bridge at six miles per hour.)

As a short-term solution to crossing the bridge, the city installed a "tipper bus" that met the Highland streetcar at Elm and Eighth Street and took passengers who lived in Wasena across the bridge free of charge.

By late summer of 1937, the city had retained the services of R.H. Tatlow and J.H. Harrington, of the engineering firm of Harrington and Cortelyou of Kansas City, to make determinations as to the feasibility of a new bridge. After some discussion, the engineers estimated the cost for a new bridge to be approximately $300,000. With this information, council authorized a bond issuance to be put before the voters to approve funding of the project. On September 27, 1937, the freehold voters of Roanoke approved the Wasena Bridge project by a margin of 1,600 to 694. Before the end of that year, council would authorize the First National Bank of Boston to handle the issuance and sale of the bonds.

In 1938, Congressman Clifton A. Woodrum assisted the city in securing federal funds for the bridge in the amount of $149,265 coming from the Public Works Administration (PWA). With financing in place, council only needed to acquire certain tracts of land to make way for the bridge so construction could commence. Only one transaction in this regard proved somewhat difficult. The Standard Oil Company of New Jersey had a filling station located at the designated east terminus. The city acquired the station for just over $6,000 and then rezoned lots on Ferdinand Avenue for the station to relocate.

Old steel Wasena Bridge, built in 1911. Photo taken in 1912. Abutments of the old narrow-gauge railroad bridge can be seen in the background. *Courtesy of HSWV.*

By August 1938, bids had been received and a small controversy ensued. Appearing before city council were representatives of the Chamber of Commerce, the Retail Merchants Association and the Merchants Protective Association, who argued that the contract for the bridge should be awarded to a local concern, the Virginia Bridge and Iron Company, regardless if they were not the low bidder. Chamber President J.A. Turner asserted that giving the job to a local business would help the local economy, create jobs and keep municipal dollars benefiting local residents. Also appearing at that same meeting was an official with the low bidder, F.E. McCaw of the Wisconsin Bridge and Iron Company. He countered that his firm had entered a bid on good faith and, being the low bidder, the council needed to honor its process. The difference between the two bids was $2,884. Council delayed a decision on the matter until the next meeting, at which point they awarded the contract to the low bidder, Wisconsin Bridge and Iron of Milwaukee. Two large contracts were awarded. The Wisconsin firm got the steel work with their bid of $116,952, and M.S. Hudgins of Roanoke received concrete and other work with a bid of $165,495. Nineteen firms had competed in the bid process.

The editors of the *Roanoke World News* affirmed council's stance. "While it would have been a source of satisfaction to have had all of this work go to local concerns, the suggestion in some quarters that the award should not be made to the lowest responsible bidder was unfortunate and ill-considered and was wisely rejected by the City Council." Interestingly, the same editorial advocated the "construction of a modern municipal swimming pool in Wasena park, with bath houses under the new bridge, to be self-supporting from the fees of bathers."[45]

Due to the inclusion of federal PWA funds for the project, the Wasena Bridge needed to be finished within three hundred days. This timeline proved difficult. When the deadline approached, only half the bridge could open. Thus, at 4:00 p.m. on Saturday, August 12, 1939, the east side of the bridge opened to two-way traffic. The bridge's forty-foot floor could accommodate two lanes of traffic even on just one side. The west side would open five days later.[46]

The *Roanoke World News* opined,

> *Opening the new Wasena Bridge marks partial completion of a project that will have immense effect on the future of Roanoke. The immediate section it serves has seen rapid growth in recent years, with probably the largest amount of home building of any area in the corporate limits…In our belief the opening of the new Wasena Bridge marks one of the most distinct forward steps in Roanoke in a decade, a step that will make for the convenience of many citizens, and that will contribute through many years to the building of a city.[47]*

The news reporter for the *World News* described the opening of the bridge in the next day's edition. "Although the bridge was not to be opened until 4 o'clock Saturday afternoon, motorists became so insistent that the span was actually opened about 3:30. Virginia Heights and Wasena buses moved over the structure for the first time at 4 o'clock and from that time on motorists came by the hundreds to inspect and cross the new bridge."

Traffic lights were installed for the new bridge at the north end, and sodium vapor lights were placed on the bridge itself. The total cost of the bridge was $331,700.

Two measures to improve Raleigh Court facilities were placed before the voters on September 30, 1938: to provide vocational training classrooms, a gymnasium and an auditorium at Woodrow Wilson, and to provide a municipal swimming pool in Wasena Park (along with a pool in Fallon Park in Southeast). At that particular time, bond issues were not presented as "packages" where a voter cast a ballot as all or nothing, as is done presently. Rather, bond matters were listed as separate projects and voted on as individual items. The $33,000 addition to Woodrow Wilson was rejected 1,179 to 548. The municipal swimming pools, estimated to be $30,000, lost by a wider margin, 1,299 to 439. Of nearly a dozen items listed on the bond ballot that year, only one, an additional $100,000 for the Wasena Bridge, passed.[48]

Harris Hardwood Company office in Norwich, circa 1960. *Courtesy of HSWV.*

On September 9, 1940, Norwich residents saw flames shooting into the air around 8:00 p.m. The illumination was caused by a fire at the Harris Hardwood Plant. Norwich had certainly seen its share of industrial fires over the years, but this blaze attracted onlookers from across the city.

Employees first noticed flames coming from the dust collector at the planing mill, a 38-foot-wide, 220-foot-long structure. With ample lumber and sawdust feeding the fire, the blaze rapidly spread to engulf the entire building. So severe was the fire that Roanoke City called upon five engine companies, which were also assisted by a company from Salem. "Thousands of people swarmed over the surrounding hills to witness the spectacular blaze in the shallow valley below, while hundreds more drove their automobiles as near the lumber yard as possible and then walked up closer," noted the *Roanoke Times*.

As fire engines raced to the scene, concerned Norwich residents poured into the streets, as many were employed by the hardwood plant. Harris employees assisted firemen as they arrived, and at one point more than a dozen streams of water were being thrown simultaneously on the structure. Near the blaze was a boxcar loaded with lumber, so a railroad engine was sent into the yard to pull the boxcar to safety. Within two hours, the blaze was controlled.

Plant manager George Wade estimated the damage, mostly due to the loss of machinery, at $100,000. Fortunately, no one was injured. Norwich, however, would feel the effects of the fire for some time as the plant, which employed 160 men, would have to be closed for three months. Wade praised the firefighters that night. "I don't see how they did it. They have done marvelous work, especially in saving other buildings, as well as in fighting this planing mill."

The reporter for the *Roanoke Times* described the eerie scene.

> *A glance at the sky afforded a memorable sight. A silvery moon shining brightly against a dark blue sky was tinted a pale red by the reflected smoke swirling above the fire and mingling against all that color were myriad sparks flying at random, some dropping on roofs of the eight other buildings in the yard. Firemen and company employees stayed on these other structures, pouring water on the roofs and stomping out sparks with their feet.[49]*

Fortunately, a positive development occurred in Norwich later in 1940. On October 7, city council formally accepted into the city's park system 6.75 acres of land that had been donated by Junius B. Fishburn. Named Norwich Community Park, the land, according to Fishburn's wishes, was to be used as "a public park, playground and athletic field." (Norwich Park was later enlarged by 4 additional acres, and, in 1968, the city built a 5,600-square-foot recreation center on the property.)

The Lakewood area was annexed into the city limits in 1942. The Lakewood Colony was a residential section of large homes that was developed in the late 1920s. The primary investor in the development was E.R. Johnson, who owned and operated commissaries along the Norfolk and Western Railway. Johnson built the first home in Lakewood about 1927, an English Tudor mansion called Lindisfarne. (Lindisfarne was sold in 1951 to Dr. and Mrs. Edwin J. Palmer, and then again in 1975 to Mr. and Mrs. W.M. Meador.) The second residence of Lakewood was a French Provincial–style home constructed in 1930–31 by Dr. and Mrs. Harry B. Stone. Designed by Smithey and Boynton Architects, this home was sold in 1952 to Mr. and Mrs. Grattan Lindsey. The home sold again in 1961 to Robert and Frances Garland, in whose hands it belongs today. Over the succeeding years since E.R. Johnson first erected his Tudor home overlooking Lakewood Park and much of Raleigh Court, many fine residences have graced Lakewood Circle and the connecting streets within Lakewood Colony.[50]

In 1943, the Shenandoah Life Insurance Company purchased land on Brambleton Avenue and shortly after World War II erected a $1.7 million Georgian-style brick office building on the site.

Two vacant lots were added to the footprint of the Norwich School property in July 1946.

Chapter 3

Postwar Development, Change and Renewal

The Roanoke City Council made one of its most significant investments in the future development of Raleigh Court when it obtained the Shrine Hill property on April 21, 1947. The Kazim Temple had proposed, and the city accepted, an offer to exchange its Shrine Hill property, containing about one hundred acres, for property owned by the city on the southeast corner of Campbell Avenue and Seventh Street Southwest, known as the W.K. Andrews homestead. In addition to the property, the city would also pay the Kazim Temple a sum of $125,000. This would prove to be most beneficial to the city's long-term interests.

In the summer of 1947, Roanoke City Council renamed many of the streets in Raleigh Court in order to create a more consistent grid of names. Thus, some street names were changed in order to adopt the name of essentially the same street on the opposite side of either Memorial Avenue or Grandin Road. On June 9, for example, Northumberland Avenue, located on the west side of Grandin, reverted to Westover Avenue, which was the street's name on the east side of Grandin. Otterview became Maiden Lane. Most name changes were adopted on August 8, with Auburn Avenue changing to Brandon Road, Lovell Road to Belleville Road, Brandon Road to Avenue, Ghent Boulevard to Denniston Avenue, Harvard Street to Oxford Avenue, Rivermont Street to Wasena Avenue, Walton Avenue to Faquier Avenue and Mayfair Avenue to Windsor Avenue. The most significant name change was Virginia Avenue to Memorial Avenue. (One should note that at this same time, Virginia Avenue in South Roanoke became Crystal Spring Avenue.)[51]

In the fall of 1947, the Virginia Heights postal substation gained a permanent home at 1418 Grandin Road. The cost of the building was approximately $20,000. This structure would serve as the post office for the area for the next eleven years.

The Harris Hardwood Company of Norwich suffered a devastating fire that illuminated the sky on the night of October 7, 1953. The first alarm was given at 11:20 p.m., followed by two more alarms over the next fifteen minutes. Some eight pumping engine companies and two ladder trucks rushed to the scene and gained control of the fire within two hours. Engulfed in flame were the warehousing facilities of the company, which consisted of three buildings each about 70 by 150 feet in size. The structures were filled with oak flooring.

The fire was discovered by M.C. Altizer, the night watchman, who gave the alarm as workers at the boiler house sounded the steam whistle to signal assistance. Clarence Whittaker, reporter for the *Roanoke Times*, described the scene in the next day's edition. "The sky was aglow before firemen got their first lines laid and began pumping water on the flaming buildings. By the time companies began arriving on the second alarm, dense clouds of smoke were pouring from the south side of the warehouses and threatening four box cars two of which were reported filled."

Workmen from the Norfolk and Western cut the boxcars loose, while pumping engines pumped water from the Roanoke River to contain the fire. City waterlines were also opened to provide additional flow to the engines. Whittaker's report added,

> As the flames shot from the buildings along the south side, hundreds of spectators swiftly retreated to safer and cooler spots. A police radio car, parked near the railroad siding, was in danger and when it was moved smoke was rising from the heated body and hood. The same thing happened to the pumping engine. Hundreds of persons were attracted to the fire as the flames visible from many sections, combined with smoke to cast a glowing pall over the Southwest section. Drivers of many automobiles found themselves trapped inside lines of hoses laid after they had arrived. Some owners faced the prospect of a long wait.

While no other part of the company's facilities was damaged, Harris Hardwood Company did its best not to halt any production activity. The company had seen major fires at its facility before, once in 1921 and again in 1940.

By the late 1940s, Roanoke City was experiencing the closing of its streetcar lines. The Norwich branch of the Raleigh Court Line was abandoned on December 28, 1941. Some form of streetcar service had been present in Norwich since 1889. The main Raleigh Court Line—which came across Memorial Bridge, turned west on Grandin Road and terminated near Laburnum Avenue—was abandoned on July 31, 1948. Officially known at that time as the Raleigh Court–South Roanoke Line, the closing of this line on that July day marked the end of street railway service in the city itself.[52]

Wheeler's Fast Service Laundry and Cleaning opened in its present location at 687 Brandon Avenue in 1950, with Vincent Wheeler as proprietor.

Major additions, notably gymnasiums and cafeterias, were added to Woodrow Wilson Junior High School, Virginia Heights Elementary School and Wasena Elementary School in 1951.

Streetcar #47 running along Grandin Road in the 1940s. This was the last streetcar to run in Roanoke. *Courtesy of HSWV.*

Gym addition to Woodrow Wilson Junior High School, circa 1960. *Courtesy of HSWV.*

Grandin Court Elementary School, circa 1960. Courtesy of HSWV.

Garland's Drugstore No. 6 opened on Valentine's Day in 1953 on Grandin Road, moving from across the street. The drugstore would serve as a fixture on Grandin Road for many years. At the time, it was the largest drugstore operating in Roanoke City. The Garlands sold the drugstore in 1969 to the White Cross drugstore chain. It would later be Revco and CVS, closing as a CVS drugstore in January 2004.

Grandin Court Elementary School opened its new facility, just off Brambleton Avenue, in the fall of 1956. Prior to this, the school had been housed in what is now the Grandin Court recreation center.

The current Grandin Road Post Office, located at 1731 Grandin Road, opened on October 18, 1958. The erection of the post office was quite controversial at the time. First, the large house that sits next to the post office had to be physically moved from the corner lot now occupied by the post office. The home was owned at the time by Mrs. Lylian Fowlkes and was purchased from her by Paul A. Wood, who also built the branch building to be leased from him. The U.S. Postal Service had a policy that all substations were to be leased buildings as opposed to being owned by the postal administration. Nearby residents, however, opposed the substation's location on the

Mick-or-Mack grocery store under construction on Winborne Avenue in 1955. The cost for construction was $75,000. *Courtesy of HSWV.*

corner of Grandin and Sherwood. A petition with 119 signatures was submitted to the city building commissioner in January of that year requesting that no building permit be issued for the facility. The commissioner, L.G. Leftwich, issued the permit upon the advice of the city attorney, at which point residents appealed to the Board of Zoning Appeals (BZA). After a lengthy session and much citizen comment, the BZA approved the construction on a 3–2 vote. Residents had staked their argument against the post office on the grounds that it would bring business to a residential area. Thus, when the post office opened, the *Roanoke Times* headline read, "Opposed Branch Post Office Is Opened on Grandin Road."

Despite initial opposition, several hundred persons attended the dedication ceremony of the new post office. Mayor Vincent Wheeler addressed the crowd, along with Kenneth Rabidoux of Washington, D.C., who was a postal official. The ceremony was presided over by Roger W. Hodnett, acting in his capacity as the district governor of the Lions Club. Hodnett had helped to start the Raleigh Court Lions Club. A flag that had flown over the postal headquarters in Washington was presented by A.D. Stover for the new branch and was raised by members of the Marine Corps Reserve: Technical Sergeant Gerald Pearce, Sergeant A.T. Davis and Corporal F.W. Evans. Music was furnished by the Woodrow Wilson Junior High Band under the direction of Frank Ramano and the school's choir, directed by Gene Ferguson. The dedication ceremony was sponsored by the Raleigh Court Lions Club, Raleigh Court Civic League, Business Men's League and Heights Club. Following the ceremony, citizens toured the facility and refreshments were served.[53]

The Shrine Hill property had long been considered a piece of prime real estate within the Raleigh Court area, for either public- or private-sector development. In March of 1958, Roanoke City Council received a communication from Dr. Walter Newman, president of Virginia Tech, that his institution had been given permission by the Commonwealth to establish a sister institution in the Roanoke Valley, to be named the Roanoke Technical Institute (later Virginia Western Community College). The Board of Visitors of Virginia Tech had appointed a subcommittee of their board to develop plans for RTI and had included among its members Mayor Walter Young. On July 14, 1958, a resolution came to the city council from Virginia Tech's subcommittee recommending that 7.5 acres of land on the southern corner of Shrine Hill be conveyed, upon which to erect the new technical institute. Council referred the matter to the planning commission.

The planning commission reported back to council the following month and suggested that the Roanoke Technical Institute be located on land on the southwest corner of Melrose Avenue and Twenty-ninth Street Northwest. According to the commission, the owner of the land at that location was willing to donate the property for such a purpose. Virginia Tech's subcommittee continued to lobby for the Shrine Hill site, however.

In January 1959, city council adopted a resolution on its first reading to authorize the sale of 7.5 acres of Shrine Hill property to Virginia Tech, should the Melrose Avenue property not materialize as a satisfactory site. When the matter was brought forward for a second reading on January 14, 1959, opposition to the Shrine Hill site had coalesced. George M. Read Jr. appeared before city council and presented a petition with 911 signatures of Raleigh Court residents objecting to the proposed sale and asking that another site be secured. Among the arguments offered at the meeting against the sale were that the action would devalue residential properties, that students would need rooms and lodging facilities not available in the Shrine Hill area and that "the institute is certain to be operated on an integrated basis, which is not desirable at a location so close to all-white public schools." It should be noted that Roanoke City Public Schools began phasing in integration in 1961 but only at three schools, none of them being in Raleigh Court. City council responded to the opposition by tabling the matter until its next meeting.

City officials immediately went to work with officials from Virginia Tech to explore other options for locating the technical institute. Finally, the matter was resolved on February 9, 1959, when city council adopted a resolution to make available to Virginia Tech twenty acres of the city farm on the southerly side of Colonial Avenue. This motion passed unanimously and seemed a satisfactory resolution of the matter to all involved. Given the expansion of Roanoke Technical Institute, now Virginia Western Community College, over the decades, this decision has indeed proven to be a wise one in light of the other options considered in 1958 and 1959.[54]

Groundwork for a new high school in the Raleigh Court area was initiated in the spring of 1957 when the Roanoke School Board asked city council to approve the Shrine Hill property as a location for a senior high school and a new elementary school. Mayor Roy Webber suggested that the request be forwarded to a committee for more formal review. The committee consisted of Arthur S. Owens, chairman; J.P. Cruickshank; and Randolph G. Whittle. It should be noted that discussions of a new high school for Roanoke had been a subject of some controversy. In 1953, for example, the William Fleming PTA had gone before city council asking that the rumors of a single central high school be addressed and, if true, opposed. Apparently, there had been some thought given to merging Jefferson and Fleming into a single school, with Shrine Hill park being the preferred location. That same year, Dr. D.K. McQuilkin, school superintendent, had delivered a report stating "that plans for a new senior high school on the Shrine Hill site be started at once."

On June 14, 1957, the committee reported back to city council providing general support for Shrine Hill as the site for a new high school. This came with the concurrence of the Roanoke City Planning Commission, which suggested locating a new fire station on the site as well. With this favorable recommendation and additional study, the city council authorized a bond referendum to go before the voters. The bond issue would be unsurpassed in the city's history relative to educational progress of the public school system. The $8 million bond referendum would, if passed, authorize the construction of two new high schools, six new elementary schools and the additions to three existing junior high schools. The vote was set for March 11, 1958.

The bond referendum proved to be one of the most contested bond issues in city history. Two groups emerged to support passage: the Parent-Teacher Associations and a group called Citizens Committee for Schools. The honorary chairman of the citizens group was none other than Norfolk and Western Railway President R.H. Smith. John Eure served as executive director for the group. In opposition was the Property Owners Association, led by Mrs. Erminie K. Wright, which claimed the new schools were unnecessary and decried the increase such a bond issuance would place on the real estate tax rate. When March 11 came and the votes were tallied, freeholders (those who owned property) had supported the schools' request, albeit narrowly, by a vote of 6,412 for and 5,259 against. It was approved in seventeen precincts and lost in sixteen precincts. According to the *Roanoke Times*, "Heavy endorsement from four of the five Raleigh Court precincts, all three precincts in South Roanoke, Grandin Court, and part of Williamson Road put the bond issue ahead. Strongest opposition was registered in Southeast, part of Northeast, Villa Heights, Garden City and Eureka." Basically, the areas where new schools were to be built voted strongly in favor.

"This is the biggest thing that's happened in Roanoke for a long time. The effect and influence will be felt for years as children grow up and go to school," declared J.P. Cruickshank, chairman of the school board.

Mrs. Wright was not so gracious in the loss. She claimed a lessening of voting qualifications had assisted the other side. Asked to explain, she firmly replied, "Women were allowed to vote by saying they own property without having to prove it." She further blamed local media, notably the newspaper, for its endorsement of the bond issue.

Roanoke School Superintendent E.W. Rushton issued the following statement on the results:

> *The interest and concern of the citizens over buildings and the education of their children have been shown in many ways. We are appreciative of their interest and cooperation in this successful effort. We shall need their continued interest and assistance as we plan the buildings and the educational program for these buildings. Now we have the challenge to develop a better school program for the boys and girls of Roanoke. In behalf of those of us in the city schools, I pledge our best efforts in continuing to develop the best schools possible.*

In its March 13 edition, the *Roanoke Times* opined, "This decision cannot bode anything but good for the future of the whole community. The vote shows that Roanokers believe in providing the best education possible and are willing to pay for it…This newspaper has been confident all along that the people of Roanoke believe in progress. The outcome of the referendum is one more proof of it."[55]

By the fall of 1959, the Shrine Hill site was being graded for construction. The school system began holding community meetings to receive input and feedback to its proposed designs for the two new high schools. The largest of those meetings was held at the Hotel Roanoke. Further, school children were encouraged to submit names of famous Virginians after whom to name the new high school at Shrine Hill. (William Fleming retained its name, with the former school building becoming James Breckenridge Junior High School.) The school board ultimately settled upon Patrick Henry. Raleigh Court Elementary School opened for classes in the fall of 1960. Also of note was the opening of Fishburn Park Elementary that same year.

Patrick Henry High School was officially dedicated on Sunday, December 17, at 2:00 p.m. The keynote speaker was Dr. Lawrence G. Derthick, the former U.S. high commissioner of education under President Eisenhower. Derthick addressed about four hundred persons who gathered for the ceremony in the school's gymnasium. The theme of Derthick's speech was international understanding. He explained that if the world were composed of only one thousand people, only sixty would be Americans. But those sixty would possess half the goods and money. He asserted that less than half the world would know of Jesus Christ, but more than half would know of the Communist doctrine of Marx and Lenin. Derthick then stressed the importance of scholarship, hard work and ensuring that students understand the principles of democracy and good citizenship. He concluded by stating that students should have "a faith to live by" and "a purpose to live for."

In eyeing the new high school facility, Derthick commented, "I want to congratulate you on this perfectly magnificent school. I have never seen a school that came so close to giving a practical application to all the educational ideas that are sound…others talk about these things, you have them."

Roanoke Mayor Willis M. "Wick" Anderson spoke briefly, saying, "The pride that all of you feel is a pride shared by all of Roanoke." Clarence M. Hawkins, chairman of the school board, noted, "This marks the culmination of years of effort by many people."

Raleigh Court Elementary School, circa 1960. *Courtesy of HSWV.*

School officials were presented with a framed portrait of Patrick Henry addressing the House of Burgesses. This gift was offered by Mrs. James Brice on behalf of the James Breckenridge Chapter of the Daughters of the American Revolution. Other participants in the dedication ceremony included School Superintendent E.W. Rushton, School Principal Harold Secord, student government President John Edwards, the school band and choir, which sang two selections, "Fling Out the Banner" and "Faith of Our Fathers." Dr. John Owen of Raleigh Court Presbyterian Church provided a dedicatory prayer.

Following the ceremony, guided tours were provided to citizens until 5:00 p.m.

The campus-style layout of the high school apparently was the result of a suggestion by Dr. James Tyson, who was then supervisor of secondary education for Roanoke schools, and supported by William Caudill of the Texas-based school design firm of Caudill, Rowlett & Scott. The firm had been contracted by the school system to provide oversight of the design process for the new high school. According to press reports, the campus-style concept stemmed "from Thomas Jefferson, who proposed separate academic halls of learning for his University of Virginia. As applied to Patrick Henry, it is a way of maintaining individual academic interrelationship with a large student body."

Patrick Henry High School, circa 1960s. *Courtesy of HSWV.*

Each hall was to house four hundred students. The *Roanoke Times* reported, "Roanoke's two new high schools were the first in the state to follow the campus-style plan. Their uniqueness even gained national attention and educators from all over the United States and Canada have flown to Roanoke to view the schools. Patrick Henry has also been designed to be highly flexible to meet a number of teaching situations. Thus space for a class of 20 or 200 can be arranged."

The new school cost $1.8 million and was designed by Smithy & Boynton Architects. The general contractor was John W. Daniel Company of Danville, Virginia. Subcontractors and suppliers included Clear-Bullock Electrical Company, E.V. Poff and Son, H.A. Gross, Roanoke Iron Works, Rusco Window Company, Tilley Paint Company, William P. Swartz Jr., Virginia School Equipment Company, Valley Lumber and Valley Metal Products.[56]

Patrick Henry was ultimately composed of four main academic halls, each of which was named for a prominent individual. (Penn Hall was not original to the plan.) Persinger Hall was named for David W. Persinger, a former principal of the Roanoke High School (forerunner of Jefferson High). Persinger also served as the chairman of the Mountain Trust Bank, as well as the Roanoke School Board. McQuilkin Hall was in honor of Dwight E. McQuilkin, who served as superintendent of Roanoke schools from 1918

Patrick Henry High School, circa 1960s. *Courtesy of HSWV.*

until 1953. Parsons Hall was named for W.E. Parsons, who served in various capacities during his time with Roanoke's public schools. Between 1905 and 1947, Parsons worked as a teacher, principal (Roanoke High School and then Jefferson High School) and assistant superintendent. Penn Hall, built in 1975, honored Dr. Harry Penn, a dentist and businessman. Penn was the first black ever to run for Roanoke City Council (1942) and was the first black to serve on the Roanoke School Board (1948–51). Gibboney Hall, a vocational-technical center, was named for Dorothy Gibboney, a former superintendent of Roanoke schools. At the time of her appointment, she was only the second woman in Virginia to hold the position of superintendent of a public school system. She retired in 1969 after forty years of service to Roanoke's public schools as a teacher, principal and superintendent. Gibboney Hall remains today and was not razed during the rebuilding of Patrick Henry High School. One other structure on the school's former campus that was named for a Roanoker was the Clara Black Auditorium. Black was a drama teacher and active member of Roanoke's civic scene in the 1920s and '30s, spearheading the effort by the Junior Woman's Club of that era in establishing classes for Roanoke's physically disabled children.

Patrick Henry High School was quickly accredited within a few months of its opening by the Southern Association of Colleges and Secondary Schools. The school had been

Transportation Museum in Wasena Park, circa 1970. *Courtesy of VMT.*

visited by the Virginia Committee of the association, which had studied the school's curriculum and faculty qualifications. Given that normal accreditation would have taken a year, Principal Secord attributed the swift accreditation of Patrick Henry to the fact that many of the students and faculty had transferred from the already-accredited Jefferson High School.

It should be noted that 1961 was a high-water mark for education in the city. Not only was Patrick Henry High School completed and dedicated, but the new William Fleming High School was dedicated on November 10. Further, the new Roanoke Catholic High School was dedicated on October 8.

While Towers Shopping Center is located outside the bounds of the Raleigh Court area, its opening certainly impacted the neighborhood and the entire south side of the city. Towers officially opened at 10:00 a.m. on Thursday, October 12, 1961. It became the first multi-retail center in Roanoke outside of downtown. A forerunner of the modern-day mall, Towers was home initially to some fifty businesses, with a cost for construction that exceeded $5 million. Its split-level design was cutting edge at the time, with the closest similar facility being in Arlington, Virginia. Plans for the construction of Towers actually commenced in 1955, with the primary investors, designers and leasing agents being in Norfolk. Originally, the proponents of the shopping center had wanted to acquire the Shrine Hill area in Raleigh Court for its location, but the city had already planned to develop the site for schools. With that land no longer an option, investors eyed the thirty-acre hill that contained the radio towers for WDBJ and considered that to be an appropriate location. The radio towers also provided the name for the shopping center.

Grading for the shopping center began in the spring of 1960. The major hurdle was not topography, but the installation of the grounding system for the radio towers. A unique grounding system was devised, using a tunnel, the transmission of which was so powerful to nearby residents and cars that radios actually blacked out.

The first tenant to lease space in Towers was J.C. Penney. In fact, their lease, signed in 1955, spurred the project forward. When the shopping center opened in 1961, the businesses located there were as follows: J.C. Penney, F.W. Woolworth, Colonial Stores, A&P Tea Company, Heironimus, People's Drug Store, Bailey's Cafeteria, Sidney's, Kinney's Shoes, Lazarus, ABC Store, Dixon's Hardware, Phillips Shoes, One-Hour Valet, Sherwin-Williams, Burger-Chef, Davidson's, Roanoker Restaurant, First National Exchange Bank, Cook's Fashions, Carol Ann Millinery, Sinclair Oil, High's Ice Cream, Ewald-Clark, Allen's Beauty Shop, Shopper's Kitchen, Playpen, Neil Good Studios, Shelley's Barber Shop, Noble's Florist, Bowles Bake Shop, Globe Record Shop, Parkers Seafood Market and Dr. James Gardner Jr.

On January 13, 1963, Roanoke added land to its park system with the donation of nine acres by the Norfolk and Western Railway. The land, located along the north bank of the Roanoke River, was connected by a low-water bridge to the existing Wasena Park and was named in honor of a past president of the railroad, R.H. "Racehorse" Smith.

The Robert Hall Smith Park was dedicated at a ceremony on Sunday, August 29, 1965, wherein the Reverend Richard H. Beasely, minister of St. John's Episcopal Church, called Smith "such a good citizen and lovable person that there was built in resistance to being forgotten."[57] Mayor Benton Dillard also brought remarks praising Smith's civic leadership. The crowd of about one hundred persons then watched as Smith's widow unveiled a plaque erected at the entrance to the park in honor of her husband.

One of the most significant developments within Wasena Park was the location of a transportation museum there in 1963. Originally called the Transportation Center and Railroad Museum, the facility opened on May 30 to much fanfare and promise. Ben Beagle, writing for the *Roanoke Times*, began his coverage of opening day on an optimistic note: "Increased tourist business and new industry were cited Thursday as possible results of the creation of Roanoke's new [museum] in Wasena Park." Later renamed the Roanoke Museum of Transportation (now known as the Virginia Museum of Transportation), the museum's opening ceremony was attended by some five hundred citizens, who heard Norfolk and Western Railway President Stuart Saunders declare that "each new project such as this contributes its measure to the total appeal of Roanoke as a place to live and as a site for new industry." The crown jewel in the museum's collection on opening day was the N&W's J-611 steam engine that had pulled the Powhatan Arrow. According to Beagle, it sat "shining in the sun as Saunders spoke."

The museum's birth was the result of a number of civic-minded Roanokers and its location and development in Wasena Park was overseen by a committee chaired by A.B. Stone. At the dedication, Stone noted that the museum was still in the process of being completed, but Stone added, "We do hope and believe it will be the best of its kind in the nation."

Another speaker that Memorial Day weekend was John E. Moore, chairman of the Roanoke City-County Civil War Centennial Committee. That committee had worked with the N&W to get the *General* to Roanoke that weekend for the museum's opening. The *General* was a Civil War–era engine, owned at that time by the Louisville & Nashville Railroad, which had been stolen at Big Shanty, Georgia, by a band of Federal raiders on April 2, 1862. After an eighty-seven-mile chase, Confederate soldiers finally recovered the engine. For the opening, the *General* pulled a 1913 passenger coach. According to press reports, the *General* drew some five thousand visitors over the Memorial Day weekend.

The opening ceremony concluded with Roanoke Mayor Murray Stoller cutting the ribbon and declaring, "We open it for your enjoyment." Other participants in the ceremony included the William Fleming High School Band and the Reverend B.P. Edwards, president of the Roanoke Ministers' Conference.

The museum was not just significant to Wasena Park, but also to the Roanoke Valley. In an editorial that appeared on opening day, the *Roanoke Times* focused on its importance. "The community owes a debt of gratitude to those with the vision and the energy to push the Transportation Museum to completion. From its beginning it should prove a potent tourist attraction."

Transportation Museum in Wasena Park, circa 1970. *Courtesy of VMT.*

The museum was funded by an allocation from Roanoke City Council and donations from businesses, civic organizations and private citizens. James O. Trout chaired the museum's finance committee during that period. In addition to numerous exhibits of locomotives, rail cars, buggies, cars and other transportation-related items, the museum had several interesting amenities. The *Big Lick Express* was a small, open-top children's train that made a nine-minute journey around the 4.5-acre museum grounds. There was also the stone Big Lick Station, designed and erected to depict a N&W passenger station. Inside the station were exhibits of rail memorabilia, as well as a working H&O gauge-model train layout operated by the Roanoke Valley Model Railroad Club. At the time, it was billed as "one of the largest computerized layouts in the South." One of the most obvious items in the collection was the U.S. Army Jupiter Rocket, which as displayed stood some sixty-seven feet and weighed twenty-two thousand pounds. Many who traveled across Wasena Bridge during the museum's presence could not help but see the rocket peering above the bridge.[58]

A byproduct of the Transportation Museum's location in Wasena Park was the development of Wiley Drive. This drive along the banks of the Roanoke River was developed as a specific means of connecting the museum and the park to the Blue Ridge Parkway. Saunders, in his public comments, stated, "We will be the only city on the Parkway with a direct, integral link to the heavily traveled parkway." According to Saunders, Wiley Drive would provide the city "a new gateway" to visitors and tourists.

Transportation Museum in Wasena Park, circa 1960s. *Courtesy of VMT.*

With the close of the 1962–63 school year, the Norwich School saw its last students. Although it was renamed Parkview Elementary School in 1959, the school had been in operation since 1921. It had suffered declining enrollment to the point that in 1962 it had only two rooms of children with one teacher and one teaching principal. Remaining students were transferred to Virginia Heights Elementary for the start of the 1963–64 school year. By August of 1964, the school windows were boarded up, as the building was a constant target of vandalism. To complete the story of the facility as a public building, the Norwich School was relinquished by the school board back to the city council on July 22, 1975. The school was sold by the Roanoke City Council on June 25, 1979, to Basham Oil Company for $22,675. Today it remains as a reminder of Norwich's earlier days. The rooms that were once crowded with children now serve as a warehouse.

In 1965, Andrew Thompson and a delegation of citizens from Raleigh Court appeared before city council on February 1 and presented a petition with 1,700 signatures advising that the present Raleigh Court Branch Library was "completely inadequate" and requesting the construction of a new branch. This effort also had the strong support of the Parent-Teacher Associations of the schools within the area. To review the matter, city council appointed a committee, chaired by Councilman Robert Garland, to work with the city librarian, Mrs. Elizabeth Drewery, on the matter. The following week, the committee reported back to the council that a new library facility was indeed needed, and that it should be sited on the easterly side of Grandin Road between Laburnum and

Raleigh Court Branch Library, circa 1960s. *Courtesy of HSWV.*

Avenel Avenues. City council unanimously concurred and decided to fund a new library building for Raleigh Court. For over thirty years, the Tudor-style building on Memorial Avenue had adequately served the library branch's needs, but increased patronage and the need to better house an ever-increasing number of volumes coupled with an inability to expand at that site meant a new location had to be acquired. The new site provided ample space for a new building, parking and any future expansion. Given that the land was already owned by the city, the council, on February 15, appropriated $105,100 for actual construction costs. A federal grant secured through the Virginia State Library underwrote 40 percent of that cost. The library was designed by architects Randolph Frantz and John Chappelear, with Frye Building Company as the general contractor. Construction began in the fall, and the new library was dedicated on Sunday afternoon, September 25, 1966.

The dedication ceremony was quite elaborate. The Patrick Henry High School Band, under the direction of Davidson Burgess, played selections from Handel and Bach. Speakers included Councilman Garland and William Whitesides, the assistant director of the Fairfax County Public Library System. Randolph Frantz and Edward Frye presented the key to the new building to Mayor Benton Dillard, and then the mayor and Mrs. William Tingle, of the Raleigh Court Elementary School PTA, cut the ribbon. A reception followed. Members of the Raleigh Court Branch Library Committee listed on the program were Chairman Garland, James E. Jones, Murray A. Stoller, Andrew H. Thompson, Sidney P. Chockley, Evans B. Jessee and the city librarian. The librarian for the newly opened branch was Miss Clover Lindamood. That year, the Raleigh Court branch had almost 3,400 registered borrowers who could select from nearly 16,000 volumes.[59]

By the late 1960s, city officials and residents realized that the old steel Norwich Bridge spanning the Roanoke River was no longer adequate. In the fall of 1969, the city engaged the services of Hayes, Seay, Mattern and Mattern to design a new bridge. The following year, the firm of Wiley M. Jackson Company was awarded a contract to build the bridge. The cost was approximately $249,000. The new Norwich Bridge was dedicated and opened to traffic on December 6, 1971.

In the fall of 1970, James Madison Junior High School opened adjacent to Fishburn Park, providing students within the Raleigh Court area a second junior high school to attend.

In the fall of 1976, the Grandin Theater closed due to competition from the new multiplex theaters in the Roanoke area. That same year, however, Rockledge Inn burned on Mill Mountain, displacing the Mill Mountain Theater. The playhouse moved off the mountain and into the Grandin Theater, opening with a summer production the following year. Mill Mountain Theater would remain at the Grandin for seven seasons.

The proposal of a halfway house for girls on Grandin Road and the pending development of an apartment complex on a residential street, both occurring in 1978, spurred neighborhood opposition to such an extent that a new civic organization was formed, the Greater Raleigh Court Civic League. This league stopped both projects and is now one of the largest and most active civic leagues in the city, with many achievements to its credit.

Raleigh Court had the distinction of hosting the very first workshop of the newly formed Roanoke Neighborhood Partnership. This partnership, an entity of Roanoke city government, was designed to develop citizen-driven plans and strategies to help Roanoke's older neighborhoods rebuild and renew themselves. On January 31, 1981, some two hundred Raleigh Court residents jammed into the fellowship hall of Virginia Heights Baptist Church. The Greater Raleigh Court Civic League's president, Anne Glenn, welcomed the group and then turned the process over to the partnership staff. Over a period of three major meetings during the next several weeks, residents of Raleigh Court identified and prioritized their primary concerns in mapping the future of the neighborhood. At that time, the priority concerns were crime, tax assessment, commercial development, water pressure, traffic and stray animals. Task forces were enlisted to implement the various strategies and many of the issues were resolved or

Flood of 1985 at Transportation Museum in Wasena Park. *Courtesy of VMT.*

improved over time. This pilot effort within Raleigh Court served as a model for many years in the work and mission of the Neighborhood Partnership.[60]

On August 21, 1983, the cast of Mill Mountain Theater's *Guys and Dolls* took a curtain call to sing "Auld Lang Syne" as they concluded their final night of their final play in the Grandin. At the end of that month, the playhouse moved to its permanent home, Center in the Square. Among the cast members that night was the late Laban Johnson, a longtime local actor and high school drama teacher. In November of the same year, Roanoker Jack Andrews purchased the Grandin and leased it to his sons. For the next two years, the Grandin Theater would serve the community as both a movie house and a concert hall, hosting such music legends as Ray Charles, John Lee Hooker, John Prine and B.B. King.

The Grandin Theater closed in 1985 due to unpaid financial bills. Appalachian Power Company cut off electricity due to the amount owed them. The theater facility was advertised in the *Wall Street Journal* and drew some interest, but it was purchased later in the year by Roanoke developer Jim Lindsey. Lindsey reopened the theater the following year and operated it for the next several years as a movie house, concert venue and art gallery. During Lindsey's tenure as owner, popular actor Bill Murray hosted a benefit at the Grandin in 1990 to assist the theater financially. At that time, Murray was filming *What About Bob?* at Smith Mountain Lake.

The Wasena Neighborhood Forum met for its first organizational meeting on July 10, 1985, thanks to the efforts of John and Libby Reed, Floyd Stanton and Ray Cross. While the impetus for organizing was to combat neighborhood crime, the forum quickly gained more positive reasons for its existence. The forum officially joined the Roanoke Neighborhood Partnership in 1986. For the first five years, the forum was known as the Hamilton-Kerns Forum, but in 1990 the civic organization expanded its territory to include all of Wasena and the name was changed to better reflect the organization's mission. The Wasena Neighborhood Forum remains active, meeting monthly at Wasena Elementary School.

The flood of 1985 was devastating to many areas of Roanoke City along the Roanoke River, including sections of Norwich and Wasena. Businesses and homes in Norwich were heavily damaged, with some industrial enterprises in Norwich suffering significant financial losses. In Wasena Park, the Transportation Museum was practically submerged, along with many of its outdoor exhibits. While the museum had been planning a location change for some time due to expansion needs, the flood hastened the need for such a move.

In 1992, Raleigh Court received national recognition when it was named a "National Neighborhood of the Year" by Neighborhoods USA. The award was presented to the Greater Raleigh Court Civic League at a national conference in Anchorage, Alaska. The neighborhood was one of only twelve finalists to be so honored during that year. The civic league and neighborhood had been nominated for their cooperative efforts in the previous year for catching and convicting a burglar in Raleigh Court.

During the 1990s, Raleigh Court, like much of the city, saw significant renovations and rebuilding of its schools. In the early 1990s, the school board, with the infusion of federal magnet school dollars, renovated its oldest elementary schools, including Crystal Spring, Morningside, Forest Park and Oakland. Also included were two Raleigh Court area schools: Virginia Heights and Wasena.

Virginia Heights Elementary School was renovated during the 1992–93 school year. Most notable for the exterior to Virginia Heights were the colored-glass bricks imported from Germany. The renovation brought the school new kindergarten classrooms, a multipurpose room and a new elevator. "And technology has taken over," reported the *Roanoke Times*. "State-of-the-art Macintosh computers will be available for pupils, and there are plans to have computer access to Virginia Tech. The library circulation system and even the school's maintenance system will be run by computer." James McCorkindale was appointed principal of the reopened school, having served at Virginia Heights previously from 1971 to 1973.

Wasena Elementary School was renovated during the 1994–95 school year, reopening on September 5, 1995. The $2.4 million renovation was the work of the local SFCS architectural firm. "The children were impressed with Wasena's new look and the huge glass-enclosed hallways at each end of the building. Natural light fills the hallways," recorded the *Roanoke Times*. Everything was in order for the first day of school except the kitchen, so the students had to bring their lunches on those days. While Wasena was being renovated, some students attended the Wasena annex at James Madison Middle School and others were placed at Raleigh Court Elementary. The principal appointed for the reopened Wasena was Roger Magerkurth.

The school board was careful to maintain the historic look and integrity of the schools while retrofitting them for twenty-first-century technology and learning. The Long-Range Planning Committee of Roanoke City Public School had proposed closing Virginia Heights and Wasena, along with a few other older elementary schools, in a report made to the school board in 1986. Citizen response was overwhelming in opposition to the idea and the plan was quickly dropped.

During the latter part of the decade, the Roanoke School Board embarked on an ambitious plan to renovate its four oldest middle schools: Jackson, Breckenridge, Wilson and Addison. Woodrow Wilson Middle School's renovation was designed by architect Richard Rife of Rife & Wood. While the oldest portion and façade of the building were saved, much of the school was razed and redesigned. The $8.8 million renovation forced the school to close during the 1997–98 school year, with Wilson students attending other city middle schools for that year. The school reopened and was reconstituted in September of 1998 for the start of that school year, with Kay Duffy serving as principal.

With the leadership of Pat Toney, the Norwich Neighborhood Alliance was formed in 1996 to "improve, enhance, redevelop, upgrade and promote Norwich." Toney served as its first president. Though she was wheelchair bound, Toney was energetic and quickly garnered the support of city officials for better attention to and improved services for Norwich. Due to her tireless efforts on behalf of her neighborhood, Patricia "Pat" Toney was named by Roanoke City Council as Roanoke's Citizen of the Year in 1997.

The Greater Raleigh Court Neighborhood Plan was officially adopted by Roanoke City Council in May 1999. Much like the neighborhood plan of the early 1980s, this plan was the product of neighborhood input gathered at multiple meetings, and it covered a wide variety of issues and desires. According to the document, the plan "establishes a shared vision and desired future for the neighborhood over the next ten to fifteen years." The issues prioritized by residents and business owners for focused attention included housing, traffic and parking, public safety, commercial development, parks and recreation, environmental quality and neighborhood organization.

In 2001, the Grandin Theater officially closed as a privately owned movie house. Its owner, Julie Hunsaker, who had purchased the facility from her brother, Jim Lindsey, in 1999, simply could not operate the theater profitably. Closing night was November 12 and the film shown was, appropriately, *The Last Picture Show*. Some 450 moviegoers attended the film as a tribute to the theater's history and tradition.

With the announcement of the Grandin's closing, a citizens group was formed that would become the Grandin Theater Foundation. On November 19, then Vice-Mayor

Nelson Harris effectively lobbied his city council colleagues to provide $500,000 of city money as a contribution to the foundation's goal of raising $1.25 million to purchase, renovate and reopen the theater. Those involved in forming the foundation included Ed Walker, Dave and Ann Trinkle, Warner Dalhouse, Dan Smith, Bill Tanger, Dotsy Clifton, Kathy Chittum, Nelson Harris and Cabell Youell. Within a few months, the foundation's organizers not only met their fundraising goal, but exceeded it. One of the most effective strategies was the selling of stars for $1,000, which now glitter in the lights of the marquis on the sidewalk in front of the theater's doors.

The Grandin Theater reopened with a private $50-per-person gala on Sunday, October 20, 2002. The theater's new $30,000 marquis read, "The First Picture Show." Beth Jones, writing for the *Roanoke Times,* reported, "When a Bugs Bunny cartoon lit up the screen in the Grandin's main theater Sunday night, the packed audience went wild delivering thunderous applause." The foundation chose Kathy Chittum to serve as executive director and Jason Garnett was hired to manage the theater. The Grandin opened to the public the next day.[61]

In 2002, the Wasena Neighborhood Forum petitioned the city to officially name a small park in their neighborhood Triangle Park. The piece of land had been called Oak Park for many years; however, it never went by its official name with Wasena residents, who instead referred to the park by its shape. Thus, on January 22, 2002, Roanoke City Council formally changed the name of the small park.

The Norwich Neighborhood and Wasena Neighborhood Plans were officially adopted by Roanoke City Council on September 15, 2003. The plans became part of the city's 2001–2020 Comprehensive Plan. With much citizen involvement, the Norwich Plan advocated the following high priority initiatives for the neighborhood: housing renovation and revitalization, physical improvements to neighborhood gateways, the establishment of a neighborhood commercial village center, better recreational use and planning for land alongside the Roanoke River and improvement of Norwich Park. The Wasena Plan had four prioritized goals: zoning, housing, better development of the Main Street village center and improvements to Main Street, including traffic calming and enhancing the gateway appearance.

The Murray Run Greenway, Phase II, was completed in 2005 in Raleigh Court, being a part of Roanoke City's greenway system that had been conceived ten years earlier. The Murray Run Greenway connected Shrine Hill Park to Fishburn Park. The trailhead below the tennis courts in Shrine Hill Park was named in honor of well-known greenway advocate and runner Dan Wright. On March 3, 2007, Mayor Nelson Harris and Councilwoman Gwen Mason presented Wright with a proclamation on behalf of the city naming the day in his honor. Other speakers included Chad Van Hyning, president of the Greater Raleigh Court Civic League; Lucy Ellett of the Greenways Commission; and Dr. Amy Rockhill of the Star City Striders. Wright, who had been diagnosed with a terminal illness, moved the crowd with his upbeat spirit and appreciation.

The Murray Run Greenway's first section had been dedicated on April 21, 2001. The greenway in Raleigh Court had been the suggestion of the Greater Raleigh Court Civic League in 1999, due to the leadership of its president, Mike Urbanski. Over several years countless volunteers, businesses and city staff worked hard to bring the Murray Run portion of the greenway system into reality.

In the summer and fall of 2005, Dan Frei made it a personal mission to clean up Lakewood Pond. Having been raised in Raleigh Court, Frei had visited the pond often during his childhood and recalled feeding the ducks that migrated to the pond annually. Over the years, Lakewood Pond had become stagnant and its banks ill kept. To bring attention to the pond's plight, Frei made a documentary highlighting the pond's ecology, history and recreational value. In response, city officials took a renewed interest in the pond, with the most notable improvement being a fountain in the middle of the pond to help aerate the water. For his efforts, Frei was recognized with a Roanoke Valley Preservation Foundation Award in 2006 for his documentary that led to the renewed interest in the pond's appearance, quality and maintenance.

The summer of 2005 saw the beginning of the rebuilding of the Patrick Henry High School facility. Several years earlier, the Roanoke School Board had assessed both of its high schools and determined that new facilities were needed to serve students. After several community meetings to gather citizen and faculty input, the board decided to eliminate the campus style of the former high school and go with a more traditional approach. The brick façade was designed to replicate the residential architecture and character of the surrounding neighborhood.

The school board retained the architectural services of Richard Rife of Rife & Wood and hired J.M. Turner and Company as the general contractor. The school construction was completed in two phases, with each phase taking approximately one year to complete. The first phase consisted of the classrooms and could be considered the "back" portion of the T-shaped school. Upon its completion, there was a simple dedication ceremony, at which Superintendent Marvin Thompson, School Board Chairwoman Kathy Stockburger and Mayor Nelson Harris spoke. The ceremony was mostly attended by students and faculty who gathered in the parking lot for the event. The school's choir provided music.

The second phase was constructed during the 2006–07 academic year and consisted primarily of the gymnasium, fine arts areas, school offices and an attractive and distinct front entrance. The total cost for the demolition of the old facility and the construction of the new high school was $54 million. The new high school was formally dedicated in a ribbon-cutting ceremony on August 20, 2007. The facility had a total of 334,000 square feet and was completed on time and on budget. Speakers at the dedication ceremony included School Board Chairman David Carson, Superintendent Dr. Rita Bishop, Principal Connie Ratcliffe and Mayor Nelson Harris. After the ribbon-cutting, those present were invited to tour the school. Students started classes in the new building on Tuesday, September 4, 2007.

In the spring of 2006, city council appropriated to the school system $4.1 million for the construction of a high school stadium on the campus. This was the culmination of one of the most protracted civic issues in Roanoke's modern history, namely the demolition of Victory Stadium. By a 5–2 vote, the council voted to put stadiums at the two new high schools versus renovating the aging Victory Stadium on Reserve Avenue. This decision allowed for what the school board had advocated, which was a "total campus" facility, meaning the school's athletic facilities and fields would be on the high school site. By the start of the 2007–08 school year, the new Patrick Henry High School was complete. The stadium was appropriately named Patriot Stadium and had a seating capacity of three thousand. The playing field, complete with purple and gold-highlighted artificial turf, was named the Merrill Gainer Field after one of the high school's former football coaches. The late Coach Gainer had led the Patriots in winning the Virginia state high school football championship in 1973. The stadium's inaugural football game was August 31, 2007, with the Patriots playing the Bassett High School Bengals. Preceding the game that evening, a formal ceremony was held at the stadium honoring the legacy of Coach Gainer with members of his family present along with players from the 1973 championship team.

On March 31, 2007, the Grandin Theater celebrated its seventy-fifth anniversary with a black tie social at Mountain View, the historic Fishburn mansion on Thirteenth Street. The dance crowd was entertained by the Charlie Perkinson Swing Ensemble.

To celebrate Greater Raleigh Court's Centennial, residents gathered for a block party in the Grandin Village on Sunday afternoon, May 20, 2007. The commercial block of Grandin Road was closed to traffic and there were many activities, live music and birthday cakes prepared by the chef of the Raleigh Court Healthcare Center. Mayor Nelson Harris read a proclamation declaring the day as Raleigh Court Centennial Day in the city of Roanoke, and then he and some older residents of the neighborhood officially cut the birthday cake.

Chapter 4

Neighborhood Congregations

Christ Evangelical Lutheran Church

The former synod of southwest Virginia first expressed interest in establishing a Lutheran church in Virginia Heights in 1915. With interest from the leaders of St. Mark's Lutheran Church, a meeting of interested residents was held on November 17, 1915, at the home of Mr. and Mrs. B.W. Kadel on Windsor Avenue. Thirteen people were present. From that small gathering, it was decided to hold weekly prayer meetings and to organize a Sunday school. A vacant store building on Amherst Street, between Denniston and Berkley Avenues, was offered by the owner, Mrs. A.C. Oglesby, for such a purpose. On January 2, 1916, a Sunday school was organized, with an attendance of thirty people. Worship services were conducted once or twice a month in the storefront. On May 10, 1916, at the home of Mrs. A.P. Repass on Cambridge Avenue, the group that had been meeting regularly formally voted to become the Virginia Heights Lutheran Church. On May 13, 1916, at the home of Mr. and Mrs. D.C. Lionberger on Westover Avenue, a constitution was adopted, a council elected, the first pastor (Reverend McCauley) appointed and an application made for the new church to become a member of the Lutheran Synod of Southwest Virginia. The church consisted of twenty-nine charter members.

The first permanent home for the church began with the purchase of a lot on Grandin Road and the construction of a small chapel, which commenced in January 1917. The lot was next to the Grandin Theater, though the theater was not yet in existence at that time. The chapel was dedicated on April 29, 1917. A few years later, the chapel was expanded to accommodate more seating and a pipe organ.

By the mid-1940s, the congregation had outgrown its facility and was in need of a new building. That decision came in 1948, when the congregation voted to construct a new church building on the corner of Grandin Road and Brandon Avenue. The cost of the new building was $200,000, being designed by the architectural firm of Thomas and Wagoner of Philadelphia. At that same time, the congregation decided a change of name was also appropriate, and they adopted the name Christ Evangelical Lutheran Church. At the time of the move, former pastor Dr. Oscar Blackwelder wrote the following tribute:

Virginia Heights Lutheran Church on Grandin Road, circa 1920s. *Courtesy of CLC.*

Moving from the little church of stucco walls and composition shingles into one of the finest stone churches in Roanoke, is a day of sadness and real happiness. Sadness, because this has been the only church many of us have known and because for many others the most meaningful experiences and friendships have come here; happiness, because the visions of charter members are vindicated, the faith and hope of those who joined across the years, fulfilled. How fitting, also, from this day forward that geographical name gives way to the greatest of all possible names, "Christ Lutheran Church."

The church facility was expanded in the mid-1970s with a large multipurpose room, new office complex, library and kitchen. The new addition was dedicated on February 26, 1978. One of the outstanding external characteristics of Christ Lutheran is the use of the beautiful Virginia greenstone. The stone was quarried from Lynchburg, delivered to the site and hand-squared by Italian stonemasons.

Between 1916 and 1991, the congregation was served by the following pastors: Reverend William McCauley (1916–18), Reverend C.O. Lippard (1918–20), Reverend Oscar Blackwelder (1920–25), Reverend James Lotz (1926–27), Reverend Edgar Knies (1928–41), Reverend John Brokhoff (1942–45), Reverend Frank Efird (1946–53), Reverend Paul Lottich (1953–61), Reverend William Milholland (1961–68), Reverend Malcolm Minnick Jr. (1968–76), Reverend Dwayne Westerman (1976–77), Reverend Paul Morgan (1977–85) Reverend Mark Radecke (1986–1992). The current pastor is Reverend Dave Skolle.[62]

Ghent Grace Brethren Church

The roots of Ghent Grace Brethren Church go back to 1885, when some of the founding members of the church worshiped at the Bethany Union Church on Williamson Road. By the early 1900s, the church was known as the First Brethren Church. In 1907, the brick church on Salem Avenue was dedicated, with the first recorded minutes of the congregation being dated November 27, 1913. By 1920, the church had relocated to Gilmer Avenue. The present site of Ghent Church, at the corner of Maiden Lane and Wasena Avenue, was dedicated November 30, 1930.

During the 1930s, the name of the church was changed to Ghent Brethren to reflect the neighborhood's name. In the 1950s, the church helped to establish the Washington Heights Grace Brethren Church in Roanoke. During this same decade, the church purchased adjoining property, the Lloyd Home, and added a gymnasium.

Since being at its current location, the church has been served by the following as pastor: H.W. Koontz, R.E. Miller, K.L. Teague, Robert Combs, M.L. Myers, Robert Collitt, Nathan Leigh, Danny Wright, Brent Sandy and Steve Taylor.[63]

Church of Jesus Christ of Latter-day Saints (Mormons)

The Latter-day Saints had a congregation in Raleigh Court from 1948 to 1984 (the present-day facility of the Unitarian Universalist church) on the corner of Brandon Avenue and Grandin Road. The Mormon's First Ward Church was built in 1948 for approximately $105,000, with members of the congregation doing the actual construction. The church building was dedicated on June 25, 1950, by visiting elder Ezra Taft Benson. Benson would later serve as secretary of agriculture under President Eisenhower and as president of the Mormon Church from 1985 until 1994. By the early 1980s, the Latter-day Saints hierarchy decided the facility was too small to accommodate the congregation, not to mention being landlocked, so a new First Ward facility was located farther west on Brandon Avenue. Thus, by 1984, the Mormons had relocated and sold their church building to the Unitarian Universalist Church of Roanoke.[64]

Raleigh Court Presbyterian Church

Dr. W.C. Campbell, pastor of First Presbyterian Church in Roanoke, was the first to advocate for a Presbyterian church in Raleigh Court. In June 1924, a postcard was mailed to interested persons in starting a new work, which read: "You and all other persons concerned in the organization of a Presbyterian Church in the Raleigh Court section of the city are urged to attend a meeting on June 5 at 8:00 pm at the Raleigh Court Methodist Church. All matters pertinent and proper may be considered at this meeting." A committee was formed to explore the possibility and potential of a new church. Committee members were J.N. Ammen, J.E. Gish, J.C. Croft, H.W. Kyler, A.O. Brown, Mrs. L.S. Wood, Mrs. J.C. Cooke, Mrs. E.H. Brightwell, Mrs. J.D. Woodroof and Mrs. C.F. Losh. Five days later, the committee reported back that 145 persons said they would join the organization of a new church. Further, it was recommended that three lots (the present site of the church) be purchased at a price of $8,750. Within one month, some $6,930 had been pledged, leading those involved to both purchase the lots and construct a temporary building on the premises. The first regular services were begun on September 21, 1924, with the sermon being delivered by Reverend Campbell. On October 5, 1924, the Raleigh Court Presbyterian Church was officially born when 155 persons were dismissed from other local Presbyterian churches to join the new mission in Raleigh Court. The church's first elders were F.A. Campbell, D.R. Hunt, C.F. Losh and G.M. Maxwell. Until a permanent pastor could be secured, the session engaged the services of Dr. Charles Smith, president of Roanoke College, to deliver the weekly sermons.

Within a few years the small, temporary chapel proved to be insufficient space for the growing congregation. On June 14, 1925, the church voted to proceed with the construction of a more substantial permanent structure at an estimated cost of $50,000. The small wooden chapel was actually moved and relocated on the existing site to make room for the new construction. The new Gothic education building was dedicated on

November 28, 1925. The beautiful sanctuary of Raleigh Court Presbyterian Church was consecrated on June 15, 1958. Constructed by Lionberger Construction of Roanoke, the sanctuary cost $340,000. The gymnasium and preschool building were constructed in the late 1990s. This church has the unique distinction of having long, successful pastorates, being served by only three pastors in its history: Dr. Zebulon Vance Roberson, Dr. James A. Allison Jr. and Dr. F. Tupper Garden.[65]

Raleigh Court United Methodist Church

The Raleigh Court Methodist Episcopal Church was founded on May 16, 1921, as a result of a meeting of laymen and clergy three months earlier. This group had purchased a lot on the corner of Grandin Road and Elmington Avenue (later Windsor Avenue) for $4,500. The presiding bishop of the Baltimore Conference appointed a minister for the purpose of founding a new congregation in April of that year. All that was needed was a congregation. On May 16 at the Central YMCA, Raleigh Court's first Board of Stewards was appointed, consisting of W.D. Wright, J.T. Bandy, C.C. Blankinship, J.H. Frantz, F.M. Mahood, H.T. Martin and L.E. St. Clair. The first worship service was held on May 18 in the lodge hall of the Virginia Heights Masons, located above Catogni's Grocery at the corner of Grandin Road and Memorial Avenue. (This is where Serenity Windows is located today, though the grocery building was torn down in the 1930s.) "The [hall] was reached after climbing a steep flight of rickety wooden steps which led to the entrance of the Masonic Hall…an unelaborate, scantily furnished meeting room." On June 15, 1921, "sign up" was held, and 101 people listed their names in a register, thereby becoming charter members. Most of the members came from the Trinity Methodist Church.

The following year, 1922, the congregation began making plans to erect a permanent sanctuary on the corner lot that had previously been purchased farther up Grandin Road. The church needed to raise $50,000 for the project. As a fundraiser, one of the Sunday school classes sponsored an appearance in the city by noted inspirational poet Edgar Guest. Ground was broken for the new building on June 19, 1922. The ceremony was under the auspices of the Virginia Heights Masonic Lodge, No. 324. The church was completed and officially opened on June 10, 1923. The building and its furnishings cost $77,000. A Sunday school building was added in 1929 for $55,000. The church undertook another significant building expansion in 1950, constructing a new fellowship hall, a new kitchen and additional meeting and educational rooms. A chapel was added in 1952.

During its first fifty years, the congregation was served by the following men as its pastors: Harris Waters (1921–22), George Oliver (1922–24), Harry Coffey (1924–27, 1940–42), G.G. Martin (1927–29), Edgar Beery (1929–32), Raymond Wood (1932–1936), Edwin Sheppe Jr. (1936–40), William Thomas (1942–46), William Watkins (1946–50), Klein Haddaway (1950–54), Bernard Lipscomb (1954–60), John Owens (1960–64), Douglas Newman (1964–66) and Richard Robertson (1966–1970).[66]

Roanoke Avenue Baptist Church

Originally known as Norwich Chapel when it was started in 1921, the congregation was known for many years as Turner Memorial Baptist Church in honor of its first pastor, Reverend Jesse Turner. With the financial assistance of the Roanoke Baptist Missionary and Social Union, the present-day building was erected in 1926. Since that time, the Baptist Missionary and Social Union has continued in various ways to assist the church both financially and with the recruitment of lay leadership. The congregation changed its name to Roanoke Avenue Baptist Church in 1989.

Some of those who have served as pastor include Reverend Jesse Turner, Reverend W.C. Taylor, Reverend Jack Gross, Reverend E.T. Hillman and Reverend Curtis Nester.[67]

Roanoke Church of Christ

According to the current minister, Keith Wagner, the history of the congregation is as follows:

> *The Roanoke Church of Christ started in the late 1940s when several people from the New River Valley moved to Roanoke to work, as well as an influx of people from several southern states. They purchased one of the large homes on Patterson Avenue for their first meeting place. After a few years they bought property on the present location at the corner of Brandon Road and Carlton. The building was finished in May 1954. In 1977, an annex was added on the property behind the sanctuary.*

Roanoke Seventh-Day Adventist Church

The Roanoke Seventh-Day Adventist Church traces its origins in the region back to 1895, when a house church was organized and met in the home of L.E. Perdue. The church's official beginning occurred in 1906, when fourteen persons enrolled as charter members. A renovated home on the corner of Thirteenth Street and Jamison Avenue in Vinton served as the first worship site. By 1944, the congregation had one hundred members. In 1946, plans were finalized and a proposal for a new church building was approved by the Union Conference and General Conference, and this initiated the formation of a building committee to explore a new site. The present-day site for the congregation at 1701 Memorial Avenue was selected, a church facility erected and the first worship service held there on August 16, 1947. The total cost of the building and furniture was approximately $80,000. A parsonage, located at 1147 Howbert Avenue, was purchased in 1950.

In 1968 a multipurpose and educational building adjacent to the church was completed. Containing a school, it was originally known as Oxford Elementary School, but later became the Roanoke Adventist Preparatory School. A daycare was begun in 1995.

The Roanoke Church has started three other Seventh-Day Adventist congregations in the region—one each in Rocky Mount, Salem and North Valley. Thirty-three pastors have served the church during its history.[68]

Rosalind Hills Baptist Church

The first meeting of ten persons interested in organizing a Baptist church in the Rosalind Hills section was held in the home of Leslie and Grace Ellis at 2642 Laburnum Avenue, in 1954. The church was formally organized on April 4 of that year at the Ellises' home, with twenty-eight charter members. A chapel was built to accommodate the new congregation at the corner of Langdon and Laburnum, with its completion and dedication service on June 27, 1954. The land had been acquired with the financial assistance of the Roanoke Baptist Missionary and Social Union. When the charter membership deadline was reached on December 31, 1954, there were nearly one hundred members. Additional property adjoining the church was deeded to the congregation in 1956 by Howard and Ida Sigmon. A sanctuary was completed and dedicated on February 7, 1959. In May 1960, the church sponsored a mission that would later become Colonial Avenue Baptist Church.

A lodge and recreational area, including a putt-putt course, were completed in September 1971. In 2005, an addition was completed (displacing the lodge) that doubled the physical size of the church. The $2.7 million facility included educational rooms, a fellowship hall with an adjoining kitchen and a connection to the original sanctuary.

The following persons have served as pastor: Reverend H.W. Connelly (1954–55), Dr. Alan Neely (1956–61), Reverend William Marshall (1961–63), Reverend Stuart Kersey (1964–68), Dr. Denver Davis (1970–79), Reverend Murray McMillan (1979–81), Dr. James Thomason (1981–88) and Dr. Tom Stocks (1989–present).[69]

St. Elizabeth's Episcopal Church

At a meeting held January 23, 1958, at the Virginia Heights Masonic Lodge on Grandin Road, an interim missions council was appointed to establish a new Episcopal mission in southwest Roanoke. A week later, St. Elizabeth's Episcopal Church was chosen as the name for the mission. The Masonic Hall was rented and the first service, Holy Communion, was celebrated on February 2, 1958. St. Elizabeth's was accepted by the Episcopal Diocese of Southwestern Virginia as an organized mission on May 16 that same year. A few months later, on August 16, the Reverend Walter D. Edwards was called to be the vicar. On April 1, 1959, the congregation left the Masonic Hall and moved its services to the chapel of Raleigh Court Presbyterian Church.

With a grant received from the National Episcopal Church, the present-day site of the church was purchased on October 10, 1959. A groundbreaking service was conducted on Palm Sunday, April 10, 1960, and actual construction began a week later. The congregation moved into its new church on Labor Day, September 5, 1960. A second phase of construction was completed in the fall of 1964, providing needed educational space.

Temple Emanuel

Reform Judaism in Roanoke goes back to the 1890s. In 1898, a rabbinical student, Theodore F. Joseph, officiated at services that were held in an upstairs hall located at Jefferson Street and Campbell Avenue downtown. By 1904, the congregation had purchased its first temple, the former United Brethren Church on Franklin Road. (This same building was later used by the Greek Orthodox Church.) The temple was dedicated in 1905. In 1937, the congregation purchased land at 112 McClanahan Place, and this became the site of the first building erected by Temple Emanuel. That temple was dedicated on October 29. By 1954, the congregation was in need of a new facility and a building committee was appointed. By July of 1955, the site for the new temple had been purchased at the intersection of Brambleton Avenue and Persinger Road. A fundraising kickoff dinner was held two months later at the Hotel Roanoke, with a goal of $150,000. Within three weeks' time, the goal had been exceeded, with $163,660 subscribed. On February 16, 1958, a groundbreaking ceremony was held at the present site, and on October 30–31 and November 1, 1959, dedication services were held for the new temple.

The theme of the temple is found in its name, Emanuel, which is the Hebrew word for "God is with us," a name symbolic of the mission of the Jewish religion. Throughout the temple are various elements symbolizing aspects of the Jewish faith. Arthur Taubman, president of the temple in 1959, wrote to the congregation a New Year Message, which read in part, "The beauty of our new structure, its utilitarian value is of course of greatest importance to us, but of far greater worth is the spiritual values that shall be inspired…I hope that in the months ahead, when we dedicate our new Temple, that the full force and meaning of our Hebrew philosophy and faith shall be brought to our children with the emphasis it deserves."

Within the past few years, the congregation has completed a major renovation and expansion of the temple.[70]

Virginia Heights Baptist Church

A few Baptist residents of the Virginia Heights section met on February 11, 1917, at the Virginia Heights Elementary School and organized a Sunday school. For several months the Sunday school held services in the school building, eventually purchasing a lot for a new church on the corner of Virginia Avenue (now Memorial) and Grandin Road. They erected a small frame structure on the lot. The lot and building cost about $3,000.

The first service in the new building was held on December 29, 1918. At that service, the Reverend Ira Knight, pastor of Calvary Baptist Church, made a motion to meet on the second Sunday in January (1919) at 3:00 p.m. to organize a new church. Forty persons present indicated they would join the new church. Virginia Heights Baptist Church was officially birthed on January 12, 1919, with seventy-nine charter members. The first pastor was Reverend L.R. O'Brien, whose salary at that time was $2,000. The first deacons of the church were P.F. Walker, F.E. Dulaney, S.R. Truman, Oscar Graves, Stuart Graves, W.F. Layman, J.R. Turner and J.F. Surface.

On July 16, 1919, the church voted to borrow $4,500 from the Shenandoah Life Insurance Company to build a brick parsonage on Virginia Avenue, which remained in use by the church until November 1948.

The first permanent structure for the church, which is the middle portion of the church complex as viewed from Memorial Avenue, was erected in 1922. The cornerstone was laid on June 22 of that year, and the building cost $45,000. In 1937, the church sold the corner lot to the Texas Company (Texaco). That portion of the church lot had been leased since 1934 to the Alleghany Gas & Oil Company for a filling station. (The church reacquired the lot in the late 1980s.) Using proceeds from that sale, the church proceeded with the construction of its current Colonial-style sanctuary. The groundbreaking ceremony was held on October 2, 1938. On May 7, 1939, dedication services were held for the new building. The final building, an educational wing farther up Memorial Avenue, was dedicated on February 17, 1963.

Since 1919, Virginia Heights Baptist Church has been served by the following as pastor (listed in order of service): Reverend L.R. O'Brien, Reverend Wirt Davis, Dr. Austin Conrad, Dr. Jesse Davis (whose tenure was from 1930 to 1968), Reverend Marvin Gennings, Dr. Michael Hopkins, Dr. Dan Scott and Reverend Nelson Harris.[71]

Westhampton Christian Church

The seeds for Westhampton Christian Church came as a result of a survey conducted by the Disciples of Christ in southwest Roanoke. The Roanoke Area Council of Christian Churches selected the site at the corner of Grandin and Carlton Roads for a new mission, and the first meeting of interested residents for forming a new church was held on March 3, 1954, in the basement of Mr. and Mrs. L.G. Flint's home, 2070 Carlton Road. With much enthusiasm and interest, the first worship service was conducted on April 11, 1954, in the Grandin Court Community Center. The first service on the site of the proposed church was held Easter Sunday, April 18, 1954. Westhampton Church was officially birthed on May 2, 1954, when thirty members signed a charter roll. For the first year, the new congregation used the Grandin Court Community Center, leasing it from the Roanoke City Parks and Recreation Department. A groundbreaking ceremony occurred on May 1, 1955, for the first unit of Westhampton's building complex, with its completion and dedication being held on January 15, 1956. The second building unit was dedicated on November 3, 1963. The third building unit broke ground on May 1, 1977. During its first three decades, Westhampton was served by the following as pastors: Reverend Walter T. Calhoun, Reverend Herbert R. Moore, Reverend Robert L. Bradley and Reverend James R. Burton.[72]

Chapel and first sanctuary of Virginia Heights Baptist Church, circa 1925. *Courtesy of VHBC.*

Virginia Heights Baptist Church chapel, circa 1919. *Courtesy of VHBC.*

Unitarian Universalist Church of Roanoke

The Unitarian Universalist congregation gained a physical presence in Raleigh Court in the mid-1980s, though the congregation's history goes back an additional three decades. In the spring of 1984, the church began exploring the purchase of the former First Ward facility of the Latter-day Saints located at the corner of Brandon Avenue and Grandin Road. The congregation had outgrown its previous facility, the former Cave Spring Methodist Church, on McVitty Road in southwest Roanoke County. On November 4, 1984, the congregation voted in favor of acquiring the Latter-day Saints' church. On November 24, 1985, a "memorial service" was held by the congregation at their former location, and then the congregants proceeded to their new home for an inaugural potluck. Thus began the Unitarians' physical presence within Raleigh Court.

The first formal organization of Unitarians in Roanoke is believed to have been in 1914, when the First Unitarian Church of Roanoke was organized, with services being held in Assembly Hall over the Builders Exchange, 119 Campbell Avenue. This congregation disbanded, however, in 1929. The next organized Unitarian work officially commenced on March 25, 1954, when the Unitarian Fellowship of Roanoke was formed. The fellowship met at the Patrick Henry Hotel. In December 1960, the congregation purchased the former Methodist facility on McVitty Road, which would serve as their church home until the move to Grandin Road.

In its first fifty years, the church was served by the following as ministers: Greta Crosby, Dr. Allie Frazier, Reverend Michael McGhee, Reverend Bruce Southworth, Reverend Timothy Ashton, Reverend Kirk Ballin and Dr. Audette Fulbright.[73]

Chapter 5

Commercial Districts, 1920–1970

Grandin Village

When Virginia Heights was annexed into the city in 1919, there was only one business listed in the city directory for that year in the Grandin Road–Memorial (Virginia) Avenue area: Reynolds Grocery. Reynolds Grocery was located at 100–02 Grandin Road at the corner of Grandin and Memorial. The grocery had opened on Grandin Road in 1906 and was owned and operated by David Lemuel Reynolds and his wife Mary, who lived next to the store. Prior to 1906, Reynolds had been employed by the S.E. Miller General Mercantile on Tazewell Avenue in Southeast. Other than the Virginia Heights Lutheran Church at 104 Grandin, all other structures were either homes or apartment buildings. The 1920s, however, would be a period of significant commercial development for the district.

In 1920, the Reynoldses sold their grocery to Louis Catogni. Catogni and his brother, James, had been well-established retailers in the city for many years. Catogni's Grocery was located at 100 Grandin Road, and at 102 the brothers opened the Grandin Road Pharmacy. The pharmacy was an incorporated entity with W.E. Airheart, president; S.V. Nininger, vice-president; and T.C. Preston, secretary and store manager.

Longtime Raleigh Court resident Hartwell Martin recalls going to Catogni's for his mother as a child. At the end of every month, he would go pay his mother's tab at the grocery and get a quarter's worth of candy free from the proprietor for paying the bill. The grocery and pharmacy were located in the same building, a large, two-story brick structure that occupied the corner and went south on Grandin Road to about where the Grandin Theater is today. The building would later be razed.

By 1921, the only change commercially along Grandin Road was the occupancy of the second floor of Catogni's Grocery building by the Virginia Heights Masonic Lodge No. 324. They, in turn, were also leasing their upstairs hall to members of the Raleigh Court Methodist Episcopal Church for forty dollars a month.

The 1922 city directory listed three new businesses in the Grandin District. At 106 Grandin Road, a branch of the Jamison's Stores had opened. Jamison's had started at 602 Fifth Street Southwest, and by 1924 there were forty-seven stores operating in the Roanoke area. The store on Grandin was number fourteen. The stores were noted for their brick-red doors. The groceries were the enterprise of W.B. and Edgar Jamison. Edgar Jamison was a director of the Roanoke Grocery and Milling Company who enticed investors in founding a chain of groceries as a means to merchandise food. The successful chain had a familiar and quite accurate motto: "There's one in your neighborhood." (The chain would be purchased by the Kroger Company in 1929.) In addition to Jamison's Grocery, two other businesses opened in the area. Samuel D. Wood launched the Lone Star Filling Station at the corner of Memorial and Winbourne, and Robert Shafer opened Shafer's Pharmacy, 300 Grandin Road, at the Maiden Lane intersection.

The 1923 city directory listed the same businesses along Grandin Road and Memorial (Virginia) Avenue as the previous year, with no additions. By 1924, however, the Lester & Graves Grocery had begun operating at 108 Grandin Road. Proprietors were Wade H. Lester and Stuart Graves. On Memorial, near the Denniston Avenue intersection, Miss Alice Howard and Mrs. C.I. Boley were operating the Virginia Heights Beauty Parlor.

By 1925, Shafer's Pharmacy had been sold and the business was occupied by the Fountain Drug Company. Still located at 300–02 Grandin, the new proprietors were D.C. Hamilton and F.W. Thomas. On Memorial, there was now the Spalding Service Company. Lyman Spalding had a filling station in Southeast and by then had opened a second in Virginia Heights.

The 1926 directory noted considerable changes to the commercial district. At 108 Grandin, there was the Graves & Cook Grocery, with Stuart Graves having taken a new business partner, J.C. Cook. At the Westover intersection on Grandin there was the Piggly Wiggly Grocery. H.F. Dill was store manager, and this was the third store for the chain in Roanoke. The others were located on Campbell Avenue downtown, and on First Street Southeast. (The Piggly Wiggly chain in Roanoke would also be purchased in 1929 by the Kroger Company.) J.F. Harris started his Midway Barber Shop at 204 Grandin, and next door to him was the Midway Pressing Shop under the proprietorship of Earl Bigelow. At the corner of Grandin and Maiden, the Fountain Drug Company had left. The building was now occupied by Garland's Drug Store (300 Grandin), with W.B. Garland, proprietor, and Everette Hawley, manager. At 302 Grandin, the Great Atlantic and Pacific (A&P) Tea Company opened a chain store with C.B. Moss as manager. On Memorial, the Standard Oil Company opened a filling station at the intersection of Denniston Avenue. Interestingly, Jamison's Stores opened yet another grocery store in Virginia Heights at 228 Memorial (the one at 106 Grandin would continue to operate).

In 1927, Stuart Graves had left the grocery business, and there was now just Cook's Grocery at 108 Grandin. In this same building (the Masonic Lodge), B.Y. Payne and W.F. Grimstead opened Bob's Luncheonette. At 300 Grandin, Garland's Drug Store had vacated and been replaced by the Clore's Drug Store, owned by Philip Clore. On Memorial at the bottom of Ghent Hill, J.H. Martseller was operating his monument business, having operated in the city for many years with a flagship store downtown. At 411 Memorial, General Ice Delivery opened a station to serve the neighborhood, being headquartered in Southeast. At 415 Memorial, J.A. Hoover was managing the new Whiting Oil Company filling station.

Grandin Road Pharmacy, circa 1920s. *Courtesy of HSWV.*

The following year, the Grandin Road Pharmacy had closed at 102 Grandin. At that location in 1928 was the Powers and Beamer Drug Store, operated by C.W. Powers and W.I. Beamer. The only other change to Grandin Road was the addition at 305 of Mrs. Pearl Woodson's business, the Grandin Road Inn.

By the end of the decade, 1929, the Grandin Village commercial district had seen significant development. In that year, even a few more proprietors came to the area. Powers and Beamer Drug Store at 102 Grandin was now Brice's Drug Store, an enterprise of Claude G. Brice. Next door to Cook's Grocery at 108 was Stanley's Grocery, of F.W. and G.S. Stanley. The former Midway Barber Shop at 204 was now a barbershop run by Odie H. Ridgeway, called the Grandin Road Barbershop. The A&P Grocery had closed at 302 and the building was now home to the Rush-Inn Tea Room of Mrs. N.E. Coleman. Alongside Jamison's on Memorial, there was Thomason's Meat Market, with W.C. Thomason as owner. With increased automobile ownership, yet another filling station opened at 500 Memorial, Red C. Oil Station, with M.K. Dupree as agent.

In ten years, from 1919 to 1929, the Grandin Road area had gone from one commercial business—a grocery store—to some sixteen enterprises consisting of restaurants, filling stations, groceries and druggists. This heightened business activity merely reflected, however, the rapid residential growth and popularity of the Ghent, Virginia Heights and Raleigh Court sections.

Aerial view of Virginia Heights in 1928. Evergreen Cemetery is in the foreground and Memorial Bridge is in the lower right. *Courtesy of HSWV.*

By the start of the next decade, 1930, the city directory noted that the Powers and Beamer Drugstore was now the Saunders and Clarence Grocery. This was the third grocery under the proprietorship, with the others being located in Southeast and downtown. Cook's Grocery had been acquired by the Mick-or-Mack Grocery chain. By 1931, the Jamison's Grocery on Grandin was now Kroger Grocery and Baking Company, as the chain had purchased the Jamison stores. The only other difference for Grandin Road was that Clore's had relocated two blocks, leaving the 300 block to go to the 100 block. On Memorial Avenue, the Jamison's Grocery building was vacant.

The listings of 1932 had the Grandin Road Inn also relocating to the 100 block of Grandin Road, much as Clore's had done earlier. The Grandin Dry Cleaners had opened at 100 Grandin, next door to the Grandin Road Barbershop. On Virginia Avenue, J. Arthur Hoover was operating the former Red C. Oil Station.

By 1933, the Grandin Beauty Parlor had begun operating next door to the Grandin Theater. On the first floor of the Masonic Lodge, Gentry E. Fields had launched his dental practice. Neighborhood Market and Produce, under the proprietorship of Berns E. Derflinger, was conducting business at 206 Grandin Road, and Mrs. Grace Palmer had converted a residence at 303 Grandin into the Shadow Lawn Tourist Home (an early version of today's bed-and-breakfast).

The 1934 directory contained three changes to the Grandin-Memorial business district. First, the Community Inn had opened under the ownership of Samuel Cooke at its present-day location. It had taken the place of Grandin Dry Cleaners, which had moved to the 300 block. Second, the Neighborhood Market and Produce had closed, and in its place was Clarence Canada's Ice Cream Parlor. This was Canada's third store

Children on Grandin Road with Brice's Drugstore sign in background, circa 1940s. *Courtesy of CLC.*

in the city. Third, the Jamison's Store at 326 Memorial Avenue, which had been vacant for over two years, had been purchased by B.C. Thaxton Grocery, with Bunyon C. Thaxton as proprietor. (As a side note, the directory also listed two businesses operating at the intersection of Guilford and Grandin: the Grandin Court Filling Station and the American Cash Market and Grocery.)

By 1935, Catogni's Grocery, one of the first businesses to operate on Grandin Road after annexation, had closed. Two new faces were in the first block, however. On the southeast corner of Grandin and Memorial, Jacob Round opened Rounds 5-Cent to Dollar Store. On the southwest corner, Virginia Heights Baptist Church was leasing a lot to the Fulton Motor Company Filling Station. Farther up Grandin at 210, the Salem Creamery had opened the Little America Ice Cream Shop, with Ray Davis as manager. With the advent of 1936, Canada's Ice Cream Parlor had relocated to the former Catogni's Grocery. The Economy Oil Company Filling Station was at 206 Grandin, where Canada's had been. At 300 Grandin, Charles Esterly was running the Virginia Heights Barbershop and Mrs. Lois Cadd was proprietor of the LaReva Beauty Shop. Grandin Dry Cleaners and the Shadow Lawn Tourist Home were no longer in operation. On Memorial Avenue, Martseller had left from below the bridge, moving to Winona in Wasena, and the property was now occupied by the Stanford and Inge Sign Company.

There were few changes noted by 1937. The Standard Oil Filling Station at 402 Memorial Avenue became the Virginia Heights Esso Station of Taylor Martin and

Interior of Garland's Drugstore at original Grandin Road location, circa 1949. *Courtesy of Garland.*

Gerard Southern. The Hoover Filling Station at 500 Memorial Avenue had become the Lyon Filling Station, operated by James Lyon. By 1938, the Fulton Filling Station at 103 Grandin had become Ward's Service Station, an operation run by Frank Ward and his son. The Stanley Grocery had relocated within its same block to 104 Grandin and was called the Caldwell and Stanley Grocery, with Samuel Stanley and Bryant Caldwell as owners. Above Brice's Drugstore, there was the Floyd Ward School of Dance. In the former Mick-or-Mack Grocery, at 108 Grandin, was Meredith's Cash Market, with Wilson Meredith as proprietor. Mick-or-Mack was at that time in the process of occupying the former A&P Grocery store on the northeast corner of Grandin and Westover. A&P would not return to the Grandin district. At 202 Grandin, Kroger had taken over the former Piggly Wiggly Grocery store, a chain they bought in 1929. At 302 Grandin, Robert Shafer's School of Dance was open for students. As the decade of the 1930s came to a close in 1939, there would be only one change that year to the Grandin district's list of businesses. Herman Ridgeway was noted as having the Grandin Road Shoe Repair in the back of the Grandin Road Barbershop.

By 1940, the city directory listed only one change in the Grandin Village. W.M. Millner's Dime Store had opened at 108. By 1941, Round's Store had become Barr's 5 Cent-to-Dollar Store at the corner of Memorial and Grandin. Gentry Field's dental practice was gone, and in its place was the Virginia Galleries, an interior design store operated by Charles Farrelly and William Figgatt. The following year, the Virginia Galleries moved to 126 Grandin, and its former space was now occupied by Kay Blanding Studio, Moran's Beauty Salon and Virginia Shafer Music Studio. By 1943, Marie Beheler was conducting regular sessions at her school of dance, and the Kroger Baking Company had moved to the opposite side of Grandin to 119. Millner's Dime Store had closed, as had Canada's Ice Cream Parlor. In 1946, Kay's Ice Cream Store was serving customers at 110 Grandin, and the Valleydale Meat Market and Bibee's Supermarket had opened at 126 Grandin. Around the corner on Memorial, the Hob-Nob Haven Restaurant was open under the proprietorship of Melvin Andrews at 502. The last directory published of this decade was for 1948, and by that time Virginia Avenue was officially Memorial Avenue and the present-day street numbers were assigned. The Hurst and Sunday Filling Station was open on the southwest corner of Grandin and Memorial on a lot leased by Virginia Heights Baptist Church. McVey Hardware was opened, and Ward's Candy Company had joined with Kay's Ice Cream. B.C. Thaxton had sold his grocery store on Memorial to Cleveland Nuckels. The reader may benefit from a summary listing of the businesses along Grandin and Memorial in the 1948 directory and their addresses:

GRANDIN ROAD: Hurst and Sunday Filling Station (1303), Bob's Place (1304), Community Inn (1308), Grandin Theater (1310), Grandin Beauty Parlor and Barber Shop(1312), Barr's Store (1314), Homewood Apartments (1315), Brice's Drugstore (1316), Kroger Grocery (1319), McVey Hardware (1320), Kay's Ice Cream and Ward's Candies (1324), Virginia Heights Masonic Lodge, Shafer Studio and Moran's Beauty Salon (1324, upstairs), Valleydale Meats and Bibee's Market (1326), Garland's Drugstore (1328), Mick-or-Mack Grocery (1330), the Virginia Galleries (1402), Virginia Heights

Kroger on Grandin Road, circa 1960s. *Courtesy of HSWV.*

Barber Shop (1406), Grandin Road Post Office (1416), LaReva Beauty Shop (1502) and Raleigh Court Tourist Home (1719).

MEMORIAL AVENUE: Cleveland Nuckels' Grocery (1736), Virginia Heights Esso (1802), Whiting Oil Company Filling Station (1828), Hob-Nob Haven Restaurant (1902), Grandin Self-Serve Laundry (1908), O.B. Caldwell Grocery (1910) and Raleigh Court Library (1916).

In the 1950 directory there were a few changes. Bob's Place had become Long's Confectionary. The Tip-Top Market Grocery had opened at 1322 Grandin Road. At 1514 Grandin, the Boston Service Station had opened as well. The Nuckel's Grocery was now the Hoover Brothers Grocery on Memorial Avenue, and the Hob-Nob Haven Restaurant was Earl's Restaurant. By 1951, Cook's Women's Clothing was doing business at 1326 Grandin, and Earl's was Gilbert's Drive-In on Memorial. In 1953, Malcolm-Seay Televisions and Appliance store was operating at 1302 Grandin, and Sherwin-Williams Paints was in place of Long's Restaurant. The Tip-Top Market had become the Shop Well Market. A year later, O'Brien's TV Center had replaced the Shop Well Market, and the First National Exchange Bank branch was in full operation at 1323 Grandin. It should be noted that during this time the Homewood Apartment building, which was located in the vicinity of the present-day Co-Op on Grandin Road, was physically relocated to the back of its lot, creating a vacant area for Kroger parking. Ellane's Beauty Shop and Shelly's Barber Shop opened at 1327 Grandin, and Mick-or-Mack moved to Winborne Avenue; its place on Grandin had become the Grandin Road Hardware. At 1410 Grandin, James Gibson's Filling Station was operating. By 1955, Harris Cleaners and Hubert Wiggington Jeweler had replaced the Malcolm-Seay Appliance Store. Brice's Drugstore, a longtime fixture on Grandin Road, had become the Grandin Road Pharmacy. The Seeds Garden Shop was conducting business where O'Brien's TV Center had been, and Ned and Helen Stogner had opened Stogner's Shoes, which specialized in children's shoes. At 1918 and 1920 Memorial were the

Garland's Drugstore on Grandin Road, which opened in 1953. *Courtesy of Garland.*

Goodyear Shoe Shop and Louise's Beauty Salon, respectively. In 1956, Sherman's Place Restaurant had opened at 1914 Memorial, and the Caldwell Grocery had closed.

In 1957, Faith's Beauty Salon was opened at 1328 Grandin, and the Hob-Nob Restaurant at 1902 Memorial had become Dairy Queen Ice Cream. In 1958, the Shower Shop came to 1506 Grandin Road, a store catering to children's apparel. In 1959, the only change was that Skyline Cleaners was operating in the place of the Self-Serve Laundry at 1908 Memorial.

By 1960, the Grandin Road Pharmacy had closed and in its place was Electric Appliances Sales and Service. The next year, Bowles Bake Shop opened next door to Harris Cleaners and Propst-Childress Shoe Company was doing business at 1328 Grandin. By 1963, Bowles Bake Shop had moved to Towers Mall and had been replaced by Bobbi Photography Studio. In that same year, Cook's Apparel also relocated to Towers with Richardson's Sporting Goods at 1326 Grandin. They would be closed by 1965. In this year, Gibson Service Station was Grandin Texaco and the Shower Shop had closed as well. Harvey's Cleaners had opened at 1902 Memorial, the former site of the Dairy Queen, which had ceased operation in 1960. By 1967, the Grandin Texaco at 1410 Grandin (note there were two Texacos at the same time on Grandin) had closed and the next year 7-11 Convenience Store was open. In 1969, the only other additions listed to the district were Grandin Road Motors at 1414 Grandin and Harwood Paint Store at 1418 Grandin, formerly the post office.

In summary, by 1970 the Grandin-Memorial commercial district was composed of the following businesses:

GRANDIN ROAD: Ruby's Beauty Salon (1302), Grandin Texaco (1303), Harris Cleaners (1304), Grandin Barbershop (1306), Community Inn (1308), Grandin Theater (1310), Grandin Beauty Shop (1312), Barr's 5&10 Store (1314), Brown Electric Appliances (1316), Kroger (1319), McVey Hardware (1320), the Seeds Garden Shop (1322), First National Bank (1323), Stogner's Shoes (1324), Garland's Drugstore (1325–27), Propst-Childress Shoe Company (1328), Grandin Road Hardware (1330), the Virginia Galleries (1402), 7-11 Store (1410), Grandin Road Motors (1414), Harwood Paints (1418) and Shell Service Station (1514).

MEMORIAL AVENUE: House of Charm Beauty Shop (1736), Virginia Heights Esso (1802), Ideal Laundry (1820), Anderson and Weeks Filling Station (1828), Harvey's Cleaners (1902), Grandin Road Carwash (1904), Skyline Cleaners (1908), Carper's Barbershop (1910), Sherman's Place Restaurant (1914) and Grandin Shoe Repair (1918).

Wasena's Main Street

The one-block area of Main Street, Wasena, at the south end of the Wasena Bridge has served as a neighborhood commercial district for Wasena residents for many years. Originally, the 100 block commenced at the intersection of Main and Howbert, and the 200 block started at the intersection of Main and Wasena Avenue. When the area was annexed in 1919, the city directory listed one business in operation at that time, which was the Wasena Grocery located at 105 Main. The proprietor was T.E. Frantz. The second business to open along Main Street was one of the Jamison's Grocery chain's stores at 101. As noted earlier, the Jamison's Groceries were a chain of locally owned stores that peaked in the late 1920s at forty-seven stores. The chain was purchased in 1929 by the Kroger Company. The Jamison's Grocery opened on Main Street about 1923. By 1926, the Wasena Grocery had closed and the property was vacant. The following year, 1927, the Miller family opened Auto Groceries. This was their second store, with their primary grocery located at 505 Marshall Avenue. Auto Groceries was located at 104 Main. In 1928, W.A. Scholz moved into Wasena at 110 Main with his Wasena Pharmacy. By the end of the 1920s, one additional business had been established when, in 1929, C.H. West and E.T. Jones opened their Wasena Barber Shop at 108 Main Street.

By 1930, the Jamison's Grocery had relocated to where the Wasena Grocery was previously. In the space vacated by Jamison, there was now the Charles Mitchell Grocery at 101 Main. George W. Grisso was operating the Wasena Barber Shop. In 1931, the Auto Grocery had become the Wasena Cash and Carry Store, an enterprise still under Leicester A. Miller. The Jamison's Grocery was now Kroger, reflecting the purchase

Intersection of Grandin Road and Memorial Avenue, 1961. *Courtesy of HSWV.*

of Jamison stores by Kroger in 1929. The next development occurred in 1933, when the Main Street Service Station was listed as occupying 101 Main. In that same year, Mick-or-Mack Grocery was at 110 Main, as the Wasena Pharmacy had moved into a new building at 216 Main. The Wasena Barber Shop had also relocated to 214 Main. There was also some additional commercial activity farther along Main Street at its intersection with Sherwood Avenue. By 1934, the Mick-or-Mack had become the Wasena Cash Market Grocery, with Peter Parsell and Stephen Truman as proprietors. Also at 219 Main was the Michael J. Stover Filling Station. This filling station, like many during that decade in the city, changed hands numerous times. The next new business listing to appear was in 1936, when the Stephen Truman Grocery opened at 212 Main. Before the decade ended, Oscar Damewood had opened a furniture repair business at 205 Main by 1938.

By 1940, there were three new businesses listed along Main Street. Gebby's Beauty Salon was at 212, Parsell's Pie Shop was at 213 and Garland's Drugstore was operating at 216. The following year, Gebby's had closed and Whitlock Brothers Painters was located at that address. They would only operate in this location for a year. By 1942, Parsell's Pie Shop had closed. In 1943, the city directory showed that the Wasena Barber Shop had vacated its location at 214 Main, and the Klensall Cleaners and Dyers was there under the proprietorship of Julius and Morton Harris. By 1945, the Wasena Cash Grocery had closed, but the Harry Ostwald Dry Goods had opened. In 1946, Pete Parcell Grocery was a new business on Main. By the close of the 1940s, the street numbers had been changed and the following stores were listed in the directory for 1948: Primrose Beauty Shop (1107), Pete Parcell Grocery (1114), Stephen Truman Grocery (1116), Ernest Marsh's Wasena Beauty Salon (1116A), Harry Ostwald Dry Goods (1118) and Garland's Drugstore (1120).

Over the next few years, there were a number of changes within this district. By 1956, Ben's Barbershop had opened at 1105 Main, as had the Wasena Snack Shop at 1109 Main. The Wasena Hardware was conducting business at 1110, but would be closed by 1957. By the mid-1950s, Pete Parcell Grocery had become the Wasena Market Grocery, and this grocery would operate for many years. Ostwald Dry Goods had closed, and by 1956 the space was occupied by the Wasena Barbershop. Also by the mid-1950s, the Wasena Gulf Station was in operation at 1119 Main. Garland's Drugstore No. 3 left Main Street in 1957. By 1958, the Wasena Hardware had closed and its former building was occupied by Circle Television, which would close there in 1963. By 1965, Ben's Barbershop had become the Main Street Barbershop, and Wasena Cleaners opened at 1107 Main.

At the end of the 1960s, the following businesses were located on Main Street: Main Street Barbershop (1105), Wasena Cleaners (1107), Wasena Market Grocery (1114), Wasena Beauty Salon (1116), Wasena Barbershop (1118), Wasena Gulf Station (1119) and Delmar Photo Studio (1120).

Main at Sherwood

Today there is a small cluster of older commercial buildings at the intersection of Main Street and Sherwood Avenue in Wasena. This area has an interesting history. The first business to locate in what was the 1000 block of Main at the time of the 1919 annexation was the Wasena Service Station at 1000 Main in the late 1920s. By 1933, a second service station would come to the knoll: the Lakewood Service Station, operated by Coy Foster at 1026 Main. For one year, 1935, Mrs. Eugenia Walker had Walker's Kindergarten next door to the Wasena Filling Station. Her space would become in 1936 the Brass Kettle Furniture Repair. By 1938, a grocery appeared in the block, the Thrift Market Grocery of Harry Cannaday, at 1016. It would operate for one year and by 1939 it was John Chesney's Modern Food Grocery.

By 1940, the city directory listed in this block of Main the following businesses: Wasena Service Station (1000), the Brass Kettle (1000), Jennings Cash Grocery (1006), Wasena Beauty Shop (1016) and Lakewood Service Station (1026). These businesses would remain unchanged for a few years. By 1943, however, the Brass Kettle would be closed, and in its place was listed Stull's Refrigeration Service. Also that same year, there was no listing for the Wasena Beauty Shop or the Lakewood Service Station. By 1945, Ruth Wise Antiques had opened in the former beauty shop space. In 1946, the Lawrence and Johnson Grocery had opened at 1006. For the last directory of this decade, 1948, the following businesses were listed, along with present-day street numbers: James Deyerle Filling Station (1902), Stull Refrigeration Service (1904), Deyerle Photo Studio (1916) and Monroe Calculating Machine Company (1924).

By 1952, Hairfield's Grocery was in operation at 1906 Main and the Friendly Lunch Restaurant was serving customers at 1916 Main. There would be no changes in this section until 1962, when H&H Plumbing and Heating opened in the space formerly occupied by Friendly Lunch, which had closed by 1960. Hairfield Grocery closed in 1963, and the following year its space was occupied by Southern Tile and Carpet. The Wasena Service Station closed in 1967 and by 1968 the Ideal Laundry was doing business at 1902 Main. In the 1970 city directory, the following businesses were listed: Ideal Laundry (1902), Stull Refrigeration (1904), Southern Tile and Carpet (1906), H&H Plumbing and Heating (1916) and James and Stoutamire Architects (1924).

NOTES

Chapter 1

1. *Roanoke Times*, January 21, 1906, 1.
2. "Ghent History, City of Norfolk (VA)." http://www.norfolk.gov/Planning
3. *Roanoke Times*, January 28, 1906.
4. Raymond P. Barnes, "Erection of Bridge Opened Wasena Development," *Roanoke World-News*, January 31, 1959.
5. Betsy Biesenbach, "Raleigh Court Timeline." Verticle File, Virginia Room, Roanoke City Public Libraries.
6. Raymond P. Barnes, *A History of Roanoke* (Radford, VA: Commonwealth Press, 1968), 184, 241, 260, 275, 276.
7. Ibid., 241, 242, 314, 321, 323, 335.
8. Ibid., 241.
9. *Roanoke Times*, December 23, 1896.
10. Ibid., August 13, 1899.
11. Ibid.
12. Ibid., August 14, 1899.
13. Minutes of the Roanoke County School Board, 1890–1923.
14. *Roanoke Times*, August 26, September 2 and 4, 1915.
15. Ibid., January 19, 1900.
16. Russell Freedman, *Kids At Work: Lewis Hine and the Crusade Against Child Labor* (New York: Scholastic, Inc., 1994).
17. Roanoke City directories, 1910, 1914 and 1920.
18. James E. Dalmas, *The Street Railways of Roanoke, Virginia, 1887–1948* (Roanoke, VA: Historical Society of Western Virginia, 2006), 20–21.
19. Minutes of Roanoke City Council, March 21, 1930, April 4, 1941, and October 29, 1951.
20. *Roanoke Times*, April 6, 1915.

Chapter 2

21. Minutes of Roanoke City Council, September 20, 1919.

22. Ibid.

23. *Roanoke Times*, September 20, 1919, and November 22, 1919.

24. Deed Book 86, 285; Deed Book 342, 305; Deed Book 221, 370.

25. Minutes of Roanoke City Council, February 26, March 17 and June 21, 1921; *Roanoke Times*, September 4, 1921.

26. Minutes of Roanoke City Council, June 18, 1921, May 27, 1922; *Roanoke Times*, December 13, 1922.

27. *Roanoke Times*, November 9, 1924.

28. Ibid., May 16, 1925.

29. Ibid., May 17, 1925.

30. Ibid., May 19, May 20 and May 28, 1925.

31. *Roanoke World News*, December 20, 1924.

32. *Roanoke Times*, August 29 and 31, 1926, November 11, 2006.

33. Ibid., April 8, 15 and 25, 1925.

34. Minutes of Roanoke City Council, August 14 and September 8, 1925.

35. Barnes, *History of Roanoke*, 674 and 710.

36. *Roanoke Times*, October 6 and 10, 1928.

37. Ibid., October 25, 1928.

38. Minutes of Roanoke City Council, May 3 and November 1, 1929, July 31, 1931.

39. Raymond P. Barnes, "Wasena-Brandon Problem Traced to Land Boom of 20s," *Roanoke World-News*, August 20, 1959.

40. *Roanoke Times*, June 7, 1931.

41. Ibid., March 16, 1932.

42. Ibid., March 20, 25, 26 and 27, 1932.

43. Ibid., October 21, 1915; Roanoke City Directory, 1938.

44. Minutes of Roanoke City Council, July 13, 1928, November 22 and 29, 1937.

45. *Roanoke World News*, August 10, 1938.

46. Minutes of Roanoke City Council, September 13 and 27, 1937, December 27, 1937, August 2, 1938; Barnes, "Erection of Bridge Opened Wasena Development," *Roanoke Times*, January 31, 1959.

47. *Roanoke World News*, August 12, 1939.

48. Minutes of Roanoke City Council, October 3, 1938.

49. *Roanoke Times*, September 10, 1940.

50. Information provided to the author by Robert A. Garland.

Chapter 3

51. Minutes of Roanoke City Council, June 9, June 23 and August 18, 1947.

52. Dalmas, *Street Railways*, 20–21.

53. *Roanoke Times*, October 19, 1958; John Keller, postmaster, letter to author, January 25, 2007.

54. Minutes of Roanoke City Council, July 14, 1958, January 7 and 14, 1959, and February 2, 9, 1959.

55. *Roanoke Times*, March 12 and 13, 1958.

56. Ibid., December 16 and 17, 1961.

57. Minutes of Roanoke City Council, January 13, 1963; *Roanoke Times*, August 30, 1965.

58. Files of Virginia Museum of Transportation; *Roanoke Times*, May 30 and 31, 1963.

59. Minutes of Roanoke City Council; Dedication Program, Raleigh Court Branch Library.

60. Roanoke Neighborhood Partnership, "Raleigh Court: A Report to the People of Raleigh Court on Their Participation in the Roanoke Neighborhood Partnership," 1981.

61. *Roanoke Times*, November 12, 2001, October 21, 2002, and March 24, 2007.

Chapter 4

62. *History of Christ Evangelical Lutheran Church, 1916–1991* (privately published, 1991).

63. Jennifer Gearheart, letter to author, July 26, 2006.

64. William Hackworth, *The Unitarian Universalist Church of Roanoke 1954–2004* (privately published, 2004), 82.

65. Betty Patrick Merritt, *The Church of the Open Door: History of the Raleigh Court Presbyterian Church, 1924–1990* (privately published, 1990).

66. Pat Hurst Matheny, *This Sacred Place: Raleigh Court United Methodist Church, 1921–1971* (privately published, 1971).

67. Nell Collins Thompson, *Association Saga: A History of Roanoke Valley Baptist Association, 1841–1991* (Roanoke, VA: Roanoke Valley Baptist Association, 1990), 208–09.

68. Information provided by the secretary of the congregation.

69. Thompson, *Association Saga*, 285–86.

70. *Temple Emanuel, 1890–1959* (privately published, 1959).

71. *A History of the Virginia Heights Baptist Church.* (Roanoke, VA: privately published, 1969).

72. *Westhampton Christian Church, Roanoke, Virginia: May 1954–May 1984* (privately published, 1984).

73. William M. Hackworth, *The Unitarian Universalist Church of Roanoke 1954–2004: Fifty Years of Service to the Larger Community* (privately published, 2004).

Please visit us at
www.historypress.net